THE
STRIPPER
NEXT
DOOR

THE STRIPPER NEXT DOOR

EMMA LEA CORBETT

AKA SUZIE Q

NEW
HOLLAND

To my sister Catherine. For teaching me what real strength is.

CONTENTS

Chapter 1

Great $$$ Potential

I am 32 years old.

'Just sit and keep quiet.'

The meditation instruction is deceptively simple.

'Just sit and keep quiet. See what comes up.'

Simple, but not easy.

I sit. But that's about as far as I get. My butt hurts. The sky is beginning to grow light as the dawn breaks in rainbow streaks across the sky.

I am supposed to be meditating. I sit. I keep quiet. I wonder what I should teach in my yoga class this morning. Maybe something that strengthens the core? I read an article last week that drew a correlation between core strength and a sense of self-worth. So if I make my students hold a plank for one minute, I'm actually improving their self-worth? That is so cool.

DING!

The bell indicates the end of the session. I open my eyes and look around guiltily. *Can anyone tell I've just been sitting here thinking?* I am supposed to be setting an example. I pack away my cushion and hurry into the kitchen of the retreat center in Bali, where I am working as a yoga and (ironically) meditation teacher.

I strike a match to light the dodgy gas stove, whisking my fingers away at the last second as it ignites with a *whoosh*. I make a cup of tea, dropping the spoon twice and hitting my head on the kitchen bench in my hurry to stand up.

'So mindful,' I mutter to myself, as I pour cereal and coconut milk into a bowl. I am starving and start shovelling breakfast into my mouth, eyes firmly fixed on the clock above the reception desk. My class starts in ten minutes. I eat faster.

The boss comes in and narrows his eyes at me. 'Are you eating?' he asks.

I lower the spoon from my mouth, chewing slowly. Suddenly, I'm not so hungry anymore.

This feels like a trap.

'If I saw my teacher eating before class, I would lose all respect for them.'

This is definitely a trap.

'I probably wouldn't do their class at all.'

TRAPTRAPTRAPTRAP!!!

He gives me one final, reproachful stare, and stalks out.

The cereal suddenly feels like wet cardboard. I can't chew. I have definitely lost my appetite. I spit my mouthful into the sink.

Feeling dark and heavy, I make my way morosely to class. I sit on a cushion in the beautiful open-air *shala*, take a deep breath and sing out a cheery 'Good morning!'

I introduce myself. 'Good morning, everyone. My name is … Emma.'

The word feels strange in my mouth. Foreign.

I invite the class to join me in a resounding chant of *Om*. There is always a moment of apprehension when I begin that first *Om* – *will the students join me?* And then a rush of relief when they do, their voices harmonising with mine.

I am distracted during the class – even making everyone hold a one-minute plank fails to brighten my mood.

I am so not yoga. I ate before practicing. I'm not cut out for this. I like breakfast too much. However much I tried to usher them away and detach myself from them, the thoughts keep rising to the surface of my mind again and again.

But as I bring the students out of *savasana* (the relaxation at the end of class) and study their blissed-out faces, I realise that the majority of them are hungover backpackers who have never even done a yoga class before. No way do they care if I ate before class.

I began going to yoga classes at the local gym with my dad when I was twelve years old. He would always stand up the front of whatever class we were in – Aerobics, Step, Pump, Yoga – and I would be right there beside him, proud of our special Dad–Daughter time. In the yoga class, I would do the poses but leave before the 'boring relaxation' at the end. Even pre-puberty, I felt my time was better spent in the weights room doing chin-ups than lying on the floor doing 'nothing'. Also, my dad would usually fall asleep during savasana – his snoring was embarrassing. The couple of times I stayed, I'd lie there glaring at him, occasionally kicking at him to try and get him to stop before the rest of the class heard.

I kept going to yoga classes on and off over the years but it was in my late twenties, when I was going through an intensely stressful time, that I began to really crave the window of peace it provided in my otherwise frantic life. The panting of my breath as I pushed my body into extreme pretzel shapes or balanced on my hands was the only way I could get my mind to quieten for a few moments. For those precious seconds, my worries did not exist. It almost felt like *I* did not exist. Just a body, devoid of any personality or sense of identity, making shapes. I would stay for *savasana* (Dad was no longer there to ruin it for me) but I would spend the entire ten minutes telling myself I would 'relax and let go in just a second, after I think about work/the shopping/dinner/what I'm doing later today.' My mind would skip from thought to thought and, before I knew it, the teacher would be bringing us up and I had wasted my opportunity to just … be.

My mind always felt like it was racing at 200 miles an hour; meditation was never one of my strong points. But once I finally started meditating, I doggedly stuck with it. Every. Single. Day. Even after years of practice, my mind still whirls, but it's not as frustrating. I don't care as much or feel the need to try so hard to make something happen. I don't feel like I'm 'failing as a yogi'.

Except for maybe when someone tells me off for eating before class.

Back in the retreat center kitchen, I make myself another cup of tea. (Caffeine? So not Yoga.) I share the boss's pre-class pep talk with one of the other teachers.

'It just really didn't put me in a good space for class.'

Good space? Oh God, when did I start doing spiritual speak?

'Well, I think you need to look at him as Ganesh.'

'Huh?'

'Ganesh. He's the Hindu God – The Remover of Obstacles.'

'He's the elephant-y one, right?'

A nod. 'Any obstacle you face holds all the divine wisdom you need to learn for overcoming it. So Ganesh himself is, in fact, the obstacle.'

'So the boss is my obstacle?'

'No, the boss is your teacher. What lesson is he teaching you?'

'He's teaching me how not to talk to staff?'

'What else?'

A slow light of realisation begins to dawn. 'He's teaching me about acceptance!'

'How so?'

'Well, it's my choice to be here, right? So I can either choose to stay here, with him and his occasionally off-putting remarks, and make the absolute most of my time at this center, treating everything that comes up as a lesson. Or, I can choose to bitch and complain about him.'

I am on a roll now.

'But if I think this situation is making me unhappy, so unhappy that I feel the need to complain about it all the time, then I should just leave.'

'Yes, but Emma …'

I don't even hear her, my voice is getting louder with excitement, 'But I can't stay AND bitch or be unhappy because it's my decision to stay. Oh, I have so Ganesh-ed that shit! Stay and accept. Or bitch and leave. Don't bitch and stay – Ganesh that shit!' I yell triumphantly, just as the boss walks in and shoots me a withering glance, his finger pressed up against his lips in an *Sssshhh* gesture.

But I don't care.

'Ganesh that shit,' I whisper quietly to myself. I smile. I look around the retreat center. Some people are meditating, others are reading, one of the other teachers is walking around the *shala* waving an incense stick. This is so very different from a few years ago, when I was swinging naked around a pole while men threw money at me. I can't help but wonder, how exactly, did I end up here?

...

'That's IT!' I screamed at Dad, angrily stomping my little sneaker.

'I was mistaken for a boy AGAIN today.' (A woman had seen the back of my head as I was looking under some bushes and told her kid to 'leave the little boy alone'.)

I was bristling with rage and indignation. 'This is the LAST TIME. I do NOT want to wear jeans. I do NOT want to have short boy-hair. I want to be a GIRL.'

Dad appeared a little stunned by my outburst, but nodded his head in a kind of surprised acquiescence. I was the first-born child in our family. I think that, deep down, Dad wanted a boy so I was always dressed in jeans and my hair was trimmed above my ears. But no more! At the tender age of four, I was staging my own mini-feminist revolution. Well, it seemed feminist to me. I wanted to express myself as a female. I wanted to be an empowered woman, embracing my femininity.

Okay, so I just wanted to wear pink and have long hair to be more 'like a princess'.

My dad was my hero. All I wanted was for him to be proud of me. To notice me. But he was always busy. So busy. Nine times out of ten, he would run late when picking me up from gymnastics or some other after-school activity. I would watch all the other kids being picked up one by one until it was just me left, making awkward conversation with the teacher or my coach. Sometimes, he would not show up at all and Mom would have to come instead. One night at gymnastics training, when I was about ten years old, I went to kick up into a handstand on the beam. As I lowered my hands, the beam disappeared entirely and I went crashing face-first into the floor. I was unhurt; sitting up, I looked around a bit, stunned. *Where had the beam gone?* I turned my head slightly. It was there, sort of. There were large white circles missing from my field of vision, like I'd been looking at a bright light or the Sun and then looked away. I rubbed my eyes, but the circles remained. Unsure of what was going on, I told my coach. He called my dad, sat me in the office and went back into the gym to continue coaching my teammates. Nausea and a severe headache began to overwhelm me as I waited. *Where was Dad?* I curled myself up in a ball on the scratchy industrial carpet, clutching my head with my hands, trying to will the pain away as I waited. *Surely he'd be here soon?* I threw up in the bin alone, no one to hold my hair back for me.

Where was he? I lay back down and closed my eyes tight against the pain in my head. And I waited. When Dad finally arrived a couple of hours later, I was pretty out of it. He cleaned up my mess and carried me to the car.

It was my first migraine.

'The only way to guarantee your father will show up is to win an award,' said my mom one day. It was just an offhand comment but I took it to heart. I decided I would win *all* the awards. I was a straight-A student. One day, I came home with an A-minus on a report card and pitifully announced, 'I've failed,' before retiring to my room to have a cathartic crying session. I became involved in every extra-curricular activity you can think of – sports (I loved being active), school musicals and plays (I loved performing), and debating and mock trials (I loved public speaking and arguing). I even asked my teachers for extra homework! I was called a nerd, geek, poindexter – but I didn't care. I loved school. And I found that, regardless of whether I had natural aptitude or not, if I applied myself and worked hard, I could do well – and win those all-important awards.

I may have disappointed my dad by being born the wrong sex, but I was determined to do everything in my power to make him proud of me. I became consumed with 'winning' and 'achieving'. Nothing compared to the warm glow of basking in his pride. Likewise, nothing compared to the bitter disappointment when he gave his word and didn't follow through.

Mom must have tired of his unreliability, too, because one day when I was nine and my little sister was six, we came home to discover half the furniture was missing.

'We've been robbed!' I declared dramatically, looking at the empty space where the couch used to be.

'We're getting a divorce,' said Mom, by way of explanation.

I promptly burst into tears.

'Don't be stupid,' said Mom.

I stopped crying.

...

After my parents separated, I would flick back and forth between their houses. I was not an easy child and things only got worse as I became a teenager. Sleep (which had never come easily) became harder and harder, especially when I was stressed by exams or too many activities on at once. I drifted towards the 'freaks' at school – I'd wear fairy wings and my Doc Marten boots in an effort to liven up my school uniform and, sometimes on mufti days, I'd simply wear my flannelette pyjamas. It was like a test. *Do my jammies bug you? We can't be friends.* Those who mattered didn't mind – my tribe, a motley group of Goths, punks, gays and musical theatre students, were my brethren. They 'got' me. They got me in a way that my family did not. My friends and I would go to The MindBodySpirit Festival, where we would buy crystals and play with tarot cards. We wouldn't shave our legs (I still don't) or arm pits (I do now). At the age of fourteen, we were sticking it to 'the man' (whoever that was).

What I loved most about my friends was that they loved and accepted me for who I was.

Completely, unconditionally.

I didn't feel I had this acceptance from my family.

For a few months, I would live with my mom, until we began to grate on each other's nerves. Then she would either politely suggest that I go and live with my father or, after an argument, I would storm out with my bag packed, announcing I was 'never coming back.' I'd then stay with Dad until things got so difficult between us that I had no choice but to go back to live with Mom, and the cycle would continue. I felt like I didn't really 'fit in' anywhere.

I longed to have my own home – a place where no one could kick me out. Renting didn't appeal to me at all, a landlord could still ask you to leave, but when you owned a property it was yours. No one could kick you out. Ever. Earning money to buy my own apartment was my all-consuming goal. From the age of thirteen onwards, I always had at least two after-school jobs – waitressing, a junior accounts clerk, shop assistant in a new age shop, life modelling, gift-wrapping at a major department store, even my own business breeding mice (later expanding into rats because the larger animals were more profitable).

I had the usual teenage-girl body-image issues – thinking I was fat and dabbling with somewhat dangerous eating habits – but when I joined a cast of *The Rocky Horror Picture Show* at the age of sixteen, my relationship with my body changed profoundly. These were the cult midnight screenings at the cinema in the center of the city. I was running around in my underwear alongside girls who were sizes 20–24, all of whom I admired and loved so much. If they didn't have a problem with their bodies, why on Earth should I have a problem with mine? The show was a highly sexualised performance, which made me feel grown-up, and the cast was so open and non-judgemental that I felt like I finally had somewhere I fit in. They even dressed like me! Docs, dog collars, long black skirts and corsets. As an added bonus, the weekly performances gave me my 'fix' of being onstage. My parents were nervous, having their sixteen-year-old running around the city in the middle of the night. But huddled outside the cinema after the show, in a big group of Goths and punks, I learned an invaluable lesson: if you look like a weirdo, people simply leave you alone. My wacky dress sense was not only a friendship test; it was like armour. Protecting me.

...

Heading into my final years of school, I agreed to move from my happy-go-lucky, fairy-wing-and-Doc-Marten-friendly public school to a more upmarket private school, in the hopes of achieving a better result in my final exams. This would secure me a place at a better university, guaranteeing a fantastical high-flying corporate role, with endless riches and eternal happiness. Or something like that.

I found to my dismay that, without changing my behavior at all, I had gone from geeky-nerd to outright rebel. There were so many *rules*. Shoes: black and below the ankle (goodbye beloved Docs). Socks: white, folded just above the ankle. Hair: tied neatly off the face (hair-ties in school colors only). The boys were not allowed to wear hair gel and if their hair was longer than regulation length, they were pulled out of class and taken to the hairdressers. The whole system seemed antiquated. One teacher actually set the debate topic: 'Feminism has ruined the happy nuclear family'. He split the room in half and, as we became convinced one way or the other, we were allowed to change sides. *This will be easy*, I thought to myself, as I stepped over to the negative team to argue against the stupid statement. I grew increasingly dismayed as more and more people left my side until it was only me arguing that of course it didn't – women weren't *happy* without the right to vote or the right to work. That was why feminism came about in the first place! With hot tears of frustration in my eyes, I stared in disgust at all the girls who changed sides.

Betrayers.

Mom let me pull out of that school the next day. I had lasted six weeks and barely slept the whole time. My insomnia seemed to kick up a gear whenever I was stressed.

I went back to my public school with something to prove. I decided to run for School Captain.

When I sat down to write my election speech, my best friend Lynda gave me the most valuable advice of my career: 'People are there to be entertained, Emma. They just want to be entertained.'

'SEX!' I shouted to a stunned crowd of students and teachers at the school assembly. I then explained I was <u>S</u>elf-motivated, <u>E</u>nthusiastic and had not one, but two <u>X</u> chromosomes. Therefore, I was singularly qualified to lead the school. I was awarded the role of Vice-Captain. I could live with second place.

Determined that I would do just as well at a public school, I devoted every spare second to studying. My Mom bought tickets to the gymnastics at the 2000 Sydney Olympics and I turned them down in favor of my books. *I'm already ahead of everyone distracted by the Games on TV*, I thought gleefully to myself. *Now I can get in a whole extra day of study.*

It's a bit sad, really. My single-minded focus meant I missed a once-in-a-lifetime opportunity.

I was a girl on a mission. I wanted to succeed and I wanted my own house. In between studying, student council, sports and my after-school jobs, I would religiously scour the 'Casual Work Available' section of paper each week – always on the lookout for new ways to earn money. An ad seeking 'Dancers and Hostesses' with 'no experience required' caught my eye – the most appealing part? – 'Great $$$$ potential.'

I've always held a strong fascination for the adult industry.

'I want to dress like her,' I said at age twelve, pointing at the television screen where Julia Roberts was zipping up her thigh-high boots in *Pretty Woman*.

'No, you don't,' came Mom's swift reply.

I loved Julia Roberts' character. I loved how she filled in a scuff on her boots with permanent marker then carried on regardless, with no one the wiser. She was getting away with something. Fooling people. Passing herself off as something she wasn't. Her life seemed exciting and glamorous. She was independent, in control and being paid fantastic money – she was living a movie-star life. And all she had to do was hang out with the gorgeous and lovely Richard Gere. I wanted her lifestyle.

Towards the end of my high-school years, I made a pact with a friend that, once we graduated, we would both become strippers in the red-light district. I'd cut out and highlighted the ad seeking Dancers and Hostesses, and took it in to school to show her. We called the number one lunchbreak, holding hands for support as we booked in our interviews and auditions. She was already eighteen; I was seventeen, but had no qualms lying about my age on the phone to the interviewer, Rebecca. Neither my friend nor I fully understood what stripping was, or what was involved, when we made that first phone call. Rebecca reassured us that 'full training would be provided.' We hung up the phone and stared at each other, wide-eyed.

'What did we just do?' I asked, before we both collapsed into a fit of nervous giggles.

I was scared but also excited. I knew that, somehow, this was the right thing for me.

Chapter 2

Getting Naked for Money

I am 17 years old.

'Strip down to your underwear and get up onstage,' barked Rebecca. I took a deep breath and steeled myself inside. This was the moment I'd been preparing for, the reason I had purchased a new bra and matching underwear a few days before. Rebecca was the Dancer Manager, who we'd spoken to on the phone. She was responsible for hiring and firing the strippers (excuse me, *dancers*) of The Club – an upmarket and exclusive Gentlemen's Club in the red-light district. She was a tough, no-nonsense type with long brown hair and a shirt with glow-in-the-dark handprints over her boobs. So far, she had walked us through our applications and interviews, and now we stood in the actual club for the final part of the day – our audition.

This was the first time I'd ever been in a strip club. No music was playing and an eerie silence filled the space around me, along with the smell of stale beer and cigarettes. The colorful swirls and patterns on the carpet looked straight out of an RSL club. Lit by harsh fluorescent lighting, it was hardly the seething den of iniquity I'd been expecting. Shiny brass poles stood on several small stages that lined the room; in the center was a bigger stage with two poles. I felt a small pulse of excitement – *This is really happening.* Rebecca flicked a few switches and the club transformed into a mystical dark pit, with sparkling red-and-pink lights that cast beautiful, swirling patterns across the stage. The poles gleamed, and music flowed out of speakers in the ceiling. It was time.

'Now,' said Rebecca.

I looked around, completely stricken. At age seventeen, I had no idea what to do; I'm here on a day off between two of my final Year 12 exams. I was a pimply redhead with a plethora of freckles and skin so white it was practically translucent. This was a long way from the exam room, where I had been writing essays the day before.

Rebecca must have sensed my uncertainty, because she looked right at me and said, 'Just pretend someone is f***ing you from behind and you're loving it.'

My eyes widened.

My adolescent brain couldn't compute what she just said. I'd only had sex once, and I certainly hadn't loved it. The other girls in my group were undressing and climbing up onto the different stages. So, I took a deep breath, peeled off my business suit (I had wanted to look professional for my interview), and clambered up onto a small stage. I gripped the pole tightly with both hands, more for balance than anything, and began to sway my hips to the beat. The girl nearest to me, Jasmine, had worked as a stripper before, so I watched her closely, trying my best to emulate the undulating movements of her body.

'When you feel ready, take your tops off so we can see your boobs.'

Aware I was being judged, but not entirely sure under what criteria, I waited until Jasmine 'felt ready', took her top off, and began gently rubbing her (fake) DD boobs. Feeling awkward and unsure of myself, I unhooked my Target-brand bra and did my best to copy what she was doing. A couple of minutes later, it was over. The lights back on, we dressed and lined up in front of Rachel for our evaluation.

'You,' she pointed to a tall blonde girl at one end of the line. 'You need to lose a little weight around your tummy – maybe hit the gym a little harder then come back and try again in a month or so.'

'You need to work on your dancing – go and enrol in a few classes, then give me a call.'

(To Jasmine) 'Just gorgeous.'

Then was my turn.

'Fake tan,' she said to me. 'Just a little bit – on your arms and your legs … and your boobs … and your tummy.'

'So my whole body then?'

'Yes … Now, let's get your names down for some shifts, ladies. What do each of you want to be called?'

Deciding on your stripper name is a rite of passage. Once you pick one, you are pretty much stuck with it for your entire career, because you develop a 'following' of loyal customers who ask after you by name. Names can range from the sublime to the ridiculous, inspired by many different things. A typical strip club will feature the following:

- Gem Stones: Crystal, Ruby, Emerald, Diamond, Sapphire
- Geographical Locations: Paris, Asia, Phoenix, Dallas, Montana, India, Brooklyn
- The Botanicals: Jasmine, Heather, Daisy, Violet, Rose
- The Spice Rack: Ginger, Cinnamon, Spice, Anise
- Gender-Neutral: Bobbi, Sam, Bo, Charlee, Sharn, Frankie
- 'Maybe that's her real name?': Katrina, Stacey, Jackie, Anne
- 'No way is that her real name!': Exotica, Destiny, Lolita, Jezebel

I was excited. I'd already chosen my name: Amber. I'd even been practicing at home: 'Hi, I'm Amber.' 'Lovely to meet you. My name is Amber.'

'Sorry,' Rebecca said, 'we already have an Amber.'

Undeterred, I try my second choice – Amy.

'Sorry, Amy is taken, too.'

Crestfallen, I try my real name – Emma.

'Nope, we have an Emma.'

What? I couldn't even use my real name. This was getting annoying.

'Fine,' I said, giving up in frustration. 'You give me a name. Something small, cute and bouncy.'

Rebecca paused for a second, and looked me up and down.

'Small, cute and bouncy, hey? How about … Suzie?'

'Suzie.' I turned the name over in my mind, before nodding slowly.

I can work with Suzie.

...

I have always been drawn to the seamier underside of the city. I loved the late nights with my Rocky Horror crew. The city at night fascinated me. It was like a completely different city emerged under the cover of darkness. The lights. The atmosphere. The hum and throb of possibility. I showed up early for my first shift after the audition. Too early – The Club wasn't even open yet. I wandered through the dingier parts of the red-light district to kill time, fingering the fabric of the barely-there outfits in sex shops, smiling to myself at the assortment of dildos and other sex toys, staring at the working girls on the street corners, and looking at the flashing neon lights, thinking, 'I'm part of this now.' I still couldn't quite believe it, I felt like an imposter, like I was getting away with something (which I guess, given my age, I really was).

By the time I got back to the club, the door was open a crack and I was shown into the pokey little change room. My blood froze as the electronic locker asks for my date of birth to use as a password. *What if someone sees me enter my birthday and realises I'm not quite old enough to be here? What if there's a live feed from the lockers to the police station to catch underage dancers?* I carefully subtracted one year from my date of birth and punched it in. After that, it became a force of habit. I ended up using the same fictitious birthdate as my locker code for the next seven years.

Amid the clouds of hairspray and body glitter, I introduced myself to the other dancers, and told them it was my first night so if they saw me doing anything wrong could they please stop me. It was very important to me that I was a 'good' stripper. That I got this 'right.' They nodded vaguely as I stared enviously at their towering stilettos and sexy Lycra dresses. I was an awkward pale child, wearing knee-high lace-up boots and a tight black dress I'd bought for $1 at a second-hand store, standing in a room full of bronzed, blonde goddesses with amazing boobs and bodies. My eyelids were filled in with blue eye shadow, my mouth painted a garish shade of red. At least I've lashed out on a 'proper' stripping bra and G-string (with side clips for easy removal), made of black spider-web mesh.

I made my way downstairs. The Club Manager pulled me aside into his office and made some ambiguous comments that, if ever I 'saw anything' going on in the office then I 'didn't see it.'

I had no idea what he was talking about at the time, although, looking back, I realise how intertwined drugs are with the strip-club scene. Much later in my career, at another club in another city, I'd frequently walk in on my boss snorting cocaine off a co-worker's breasts. He always offered me some. I always politely declined.

I don't remember feeling particularly nervous that first time – just the desire to do a 'good job'.

'I can do this,' I repeated silently to myself, as I danced onstage for my first podium, where customers put tipping dollars into my garter. I tried my best to remember a few of Jasmine's body movements at my audition. I did the ones I recalled, and then I did them again. I took my top off and did them again. The whole time I kept repeating to myself: *I'm hot; I'm gorgeous; I can do this*, in my head. Then in a moment, I dropped my mantra and began to think, *Oh my God, what the hell am I doing?* The illusion began to slip. My movements became awkward, clunky. Whatever I was thinking projected outwards to my customers, so I learn to fake it until I could make it. I befriended a group of four men sitting close to the stage, who were delighted to learn this was not only my first night – but my first-ever podium! They called it my 'initiation' and, as I clambered down from the stage, they formed a protective circle around me and herded me to reception to book me for my first-ever Private Show.

These shows were held in smaller rooms towards the back of the club. A security guard walked us down a dimly lit corridor to an empty room that was to be mine for the entire duration of my fifteen-minute Private Show. It was partitioned off from the other rooms by sheer curtains and contained a small podium, no bigger than a coffee table, and couches for the customers. If you were completely dressed, you could sit on the couch beside the customer, but as soon as you began to disrobe you had to stay on the podium, arms and legs contained within its invisible boundaries. Whereas on the main stage you could be topless only, Privates were full nude and they were where the big money was to be made.

'No touching, you understand?' the burly security guard said, as he ushered us inside. 'You keep yourselves

one metre away from her at all times. I will be watching.'
He pointed to the little dome of glass in the top corner
of the room that contained a security camera, providing
a live feed from each room back to the office. On his
way out, he locked eyes with me and raised his eyebrows
slightly, asking if I was okay. I nodded gamely, hoping I
looked a lot braver than I felt.

'They do *anything*. They try to touch you. You leave,
okay? I'll look after you.'

I nodded again. Actually feeling a little braver now.

'We're breaking you in,' joked the tall gangly man in
a Hawaiian print shirt, as I arranged them all on the two
couches facing the small stage and took a deep breath.

'Here we go!' I announced cheerfully.

They all clapped and hooted and whistled.

I writhed around onstage, played with my boobs and
parted my legs for them. I was still working part-time in
the gift-wrapping department of a large store. In that
job, I wrapped presents. At The Club, I was the present.
I unwrapped myself and showed men parts of my
body. All the parts of my body. I had no qualms about
showing off my private parts. They might as well have
been looking into my inner ear. I didn't feel particularly
excited. I was definitely not turned on. I chatted happily,
while trying to glance surreptitiously at my watch every
now and then to see how I was going for time.

They told me my body was beautiful and said those
magic words, 'You're doing great.'

I beamed.

I had been given a room at the very end of the club,

with a window that faced the street. When I was bent over with my butt to the customers (so they were suitably distracted), I twitched the heavy red velvet curtains apart with my fingers, just enough so I could peek through the crack into the real world outside. Already, it looked different, almost unreal. Like the real world was inside the darkened womb of The Club. Cars passed by on the road outside – only metres from where I was dancing naked in front of a group of strangers. I wondered if the drivers had any idea what was happening just behind the glass and curtains that separated us. It was not only the world outside that looked different. Already, I felt different, too. I felt like I could fit in here. I'd sensed this was for me, but wondered if I could actually do it. I thought, *I really could.*

At the end of the group show, Hawaiian Shirt said he would like to book me for another show – just me and him. At first I was happy. *I had done well!* Then I felt worried. I only had a limited repertoire of sexy moves; he was just going to see the same thing, the same parts of me, in the same way. He did and he didn't care – he loved it and booked me for a third dance. Then one of the other guys booked me. I did the same show. Then another guy, then Hawaiian Shirt again. By the time I'd performed the same striptease for each of those four men, my fifteen-minute routine was down pat and I now knew that, not only could I do this, but I could be good at it. Really good. I was smiling to myself on my way back to the change room to freshen up after that first wave of Privates, when some familiar white dots started dancing in front of my eyes. *Not now. Not now. Not now.*

I couldn't have a migraine right now. I just couldn't .

Hoping it was just the strobe lights playing with my vision, I continued upstairs, but they didn't disappear. I was called onstage just as the long icy fingers of pain start snaking their way up the back of my skull. I only just made it through my fifteen-minute podium (the whole time thinking, *Oh my God, what if it's the lights here that set me off? What if I'm allergic to strip-club lights? Maybe this is a sign? Maybe I'm not meant to be doing this?* Before stumbling upstairs and emptying my guts into the toilet.

I explained myself and my migraine to the receptionist, who benevolently granted me an early mark. I was stunned when she slid a pile of fifties into my hand. Despite only completing half a shift, I had made $357. To my seventeen-year-old self, who had spent the earlier part of the day gift-wrapping, this was a small fortune! This would vastly speed up my savings for my apartment deposit.

I got the security guard to walk me out of The Club and into a waiting taxi. Leaving the safety of The Club is when I felt most vulnerable – out in the real world – I felt much more protected with a six-foot tall (and almost as wide) Tongan man beside me.

'Make sure you never leave with a customer, ya?' he said through the open window. 'It'll look like you've solicited them, and we get a big fine.'

I nodded weakly and slumped my aching head against the window frame. On the way home, I pulled out my wallet and fingered the wad of fifties inside. I decided that, migraine or not, this was the way to get my apartment. This was actually … fun.

There are some serious perks to working in Gentlemen's Clubs. Firstly, the compliments – any lingering issues I may have had about my body were quickly dispersed by hundreds of strangers telling me how beautiful I was each week. Men complimented my pale skin, my little pot belly, and my natural boobs. The fact is, men just like naked women. Naked women who are willing to talk and flirt with them.

The money was (usually) great and I got to have conversations with some very high profile and successful men. (Anyone who can afford $500 each week just to spend a few hours with me have been doing something right financially.) Meeting so many different people from so many different professions was fascinating.

'Hi, I'm Suzie – mind if I sit down?'

'Sure.'

'What do you do?'

The answers range from real estate agent, CEO, someone who sorted recycling, insurance broker, someone from the Attorney General's Office and even a man who designed carpets.

'Do you like it?' I asked.

'Meh, it's a job,' they shrugged in reply.

I do the maths quickly in my head – you spend at least 40 hours a week at work, plus a few hours commuting. So, say, 188 hours a month, which adds up to 2256 hours a year. That's an awful lot of time doing something you don't love. About 50 per cent of your waking hours, in fact. I promised myself that I would never, ever, dedicate that much of my life to something unless I absolutely loved it. And it was safe to say, I loved stripping. Once you got your head around the fact you were naked, then really, all you were doing was dancing, drinking and chatting with people. It was good money, considering my limited skillset. All those school plays and musicals had been invaluable for my stage presence. As were my gymnastics skills (naked handstands never fail to impress the guys).

I enjoyed the chatting almost as much as I loved the performing. It was fun finding out about all these different people – what they did, what they liked, how they felt about life. I was not a 'wham bam, thank you Ma'am' kind of stripper. I wanted to get to know my customers. I liked L-O-N-G Privates. I'd show a man the inside walls of my vagina while trying to engage him in conversation. At the end of that first fifteen-minute interval, one of the hostesses appeared. Hostesses manage the Private rooms on busy nights (when the security guards were occupied elsewhere) and fill in as waitresses when The Club was quieter. She poked her head around the curtain and asked if he, 'Would like to extend?'

This was usually followed by some bawdy remark by the customer, like 'I already have, har har har.' She and I surreptitiously rolled our eyes at each other and then I held my breath nervously. *Had I done my job right? Had I created a perfect magic bubble that he did not want to leave?* If we didn't connect, the show finished and I went out to the floor, methodically approaching table after table of men until someone else agreed to a show and I repeat the process over again. If we did connect and he agreed to extend the show, I did a little internal fist pump. *YES*.

Once we had our 'connection', it was up to me to convince him to stay for as long as possible – sometimes up to five hours at a time. People don't realise that stripping isn't a dancing job; it's a talking job. Sometimes the conversations are banal, predictable; sometimes I try to make the conversation as ridiculous as possible – just to give them a more memorable night:

'Have you ever had sex on a trampoline?'

'No.'

'Oh I have – it's amazing! Once you get the bounce going, it does half the work for you.'

Sometimes we connected on a deeper level – discussing everything from Unit Trusts to true love and the meaning of life. I don't care how special your vagina is (and some girls try very hard to have a special one – dying their pubic hair, shaving it into heart shapes or vajazzling it with diamantes) – it's your ability to engage them in conversation that's going to keep them entertained for hours. The high earners of the club aren't the prettiest girls, or the girls with the biggest boobs; it's the girls who have the ability to talk. The main skill I gained from my time table-dancing was the ability to talk to anybody at any time about anything. I believed that every person I encountered had something to teach me and I was determined to discover what that was.

Also, I got really good at taking my clothes off.

My customers were predominately male. Occasionally a man came in with his girlfriend or wife. Usually, it was the gentleman's idea to bring his partner to a strip club; she was feeling slightly uncomfortable. I always lavished my attention on the female of the pair. This assuaged her discomfort, made her feel less jealous and also indulged her partner's girl-on-girl/threesome fantasy that had brought him into the club in the first place. Girls seem to feel uncomfortable about strip clubs – but I think it's the one club you can confidently send your partner into, knowing he has very little chance of picking up!

I was only once booked for a Private by a solo female customer. We actually ended up dating for a short time. She was a masseuse at a sensual massage boutique in the inner west. We joke that I gave my customers blue balls while she always delivered a happy ending.

When I think about it, there must be an enormous amount of sexual frustration that comes from being at a strip club, where you can look but never touch. Is it a test of self-control? And yet, there are men who come back night after night after night. Treating the place almost like it's their local pub. They're the 'regulars' of the club. We called them the Bar Flies because they were always hovering around the bar.

Despite it technically being against the rules, I did occasionally venture out of The Club with regular customers. Freddy was a high roller who never went for Private shows, but paid for you to sit at his table in the 'Diamond Room' and entertain his friends during his extravagant client luncheons. The Diamond Room was the function room of The Club, where customers paid a premium to be served elaborate seafood platters and watch full nude Feature Shows performed by professional showgirls.

For us 'regular' girls, nudity was compulsory on podiums in the Diamond Room, which made selling Privates a challenge – you had to try and convince a customer to pay for what he'd technically already seen for free. It was sometimes hard to keep focused on closing your sale when you were fully naked beside a platter of oysters, lobsters and prawns, fending off inappropriate comments about seafood …

Sometimes Freddy took a bunch of us girls out with him in the evening – we got paid $500 each to go and hang out at a Piano Bar with him and his crew, drinking, chatting and dancing. Nothing else ever happened; I think they just liked having pretty girls to hang out with. Often it was a scramble in the change room, as we pooled clothing resources to put together an appropriate 'going out' outfit.

'Ahhh, I only have sneakers, do you think I can wear my clear six-inch heels under my jeans?'

'If I borrow your pants and then wear my dress as a top – does this look okay?'

Because of the environment in which we were working, strippers have an instant sense of intimacy and shared knowledge. The camaraderie in a strip-club change room is like nothing else I've ever experienced. Where else could you bend over naked in front of a co-worker and ask, 'Can you see my tampon string?' Toilet doors were never closed so we chatted while we were peeing, and sometimes we were booked together for 'Double Shows' (where a customer booked two girls at once). It was always a laugh when you were booked with a friend – we'd giggle, brush our hands over each other's boobs and pretend to go down on each other (long hair was helpful here) – the 'No Touching' rule technically applied to us as well. Sometimes I was booked with a girl who I didn't know that well, or at all, and we would both feel a little awkward. Wondering, *Is she okay if I accidentally touch her boobs?* Or, *I hope she knows the hair trick. I don't want to get into trouble with management.* Being thrown together like this meant we got to know the intimate details of each other's bodies – but often very little about our real lives outside The Club.

Even outside of work, we always referred to each other by our dancer names. To use another girl's real name without explicit invitation was a huge sign of disrespect. In The Club, there was still an element of competition between the dancers and you didn't want a jealous girl to announce to your cashed-up regular that you were actually married with two kids, and blab out your real name – thereby negating whatever (perceived) chance he thought he may have had with you.

Despite this competitive edge, we were all fiercely protective of each other. I was once performing a Private and the guy slapped me on the butt – hard – as I climbed up onto the podium. I yelled out 'Oi!' at the top my lungs and there were two dancer friends and a security guard at the door within seconds. The Club was a perfect bubble of safety and protection. Ever keen to appear 'professional', I opted to bite my tongue and finish the show, seething with a simmering rage while I tried to act interested and flirty with the awful man who had violated the basic 'No Touching' rule.

Men came into the club knowing that they couldn't touch us or sleep with us – but that veil of unavailability was interpreted as a challenge by some, who tried anything and everything to go further. If you want sex, go to a brothel. Don't get annoyed at a stripper when she tells you that you can't touch her. You just can't. She gets a fine. The club gets a fine. In fact, everyone except the touchy customer who broke the rules in the first place gets a fine. How do they catch you? Well, occasionally, cops (always at least three and almost invariably male) casually dropped in – they would stay for about half an hour, just to make sure nothing untoward was going on.

Jasmine almost caused a riot once – her arms encircling a young cop and gripping his gun in his holster, whispering, 'Is that a gun in your pocket?' in his ear.

He was not impressed.

Some of the girls really got into their stripper personas. In real life, Jasmine was a law student who was sweet and shy, no way would she have tried anything like that outside The Club! Here was where we could live out our most outrageous selves without repercussions. I tried not to socialise too much with the other dancers while we were at work; it wasn't the same as interacting with someone's 'real self'. It was fake. Besides, a group of women drinking and cackling while huddled around the bar together is as intimidating to men inside the contrived environment of a strip club as it is in out in a regular bar or nightclub. I methodically worked my way around the tables in the club until I sold someone a Private Show.

I sometimes eavesdropped on the other dancers – some of the girls often flatted together and the change room was like a naked version of Flatmate Finder. I guess it was easier than trying to explain your irregular hours, unusual clothes and lifestyle to a 'normal' flatmate. I was still living at home. Mom was easily tricked; she thought I was waiting tables at a nameless 24-hour cafe in the city. When she was out, I practiced walking in my six-inch heels, bought second-hand from another dancer for $10. At first, I was like a baby gazelle, struggling to walk for the first time, but I persevered. Practicing and working hard will make you better at anything and I tottered determinedly around the house, doing the washing and vacuuming.

I listened to these conversations between my cohabitating co-workers with a kind of jealous awe. How nice it would be to be able to dry my freshly washed stripper wear outside on the clothesline, rather than in my dark cupboard. Although my lycra evening gowns and glittery G-strings would look quite incongruous flapping in the breeze alongside Mom's tea towels and nightgowns.

One night two girls were discussing the rent on a luxury apartment that they were proposing to rent together

'It's eight hundred dollars a week. So four hundred each.'

'Oh my god, that's eight Privates, just to cover the rent!' (Everything in the stripper economy is calculated in 'How many Privates?' 'I love that dress. Ah, it's just three Privates! I'll take it!').

'But we're living *the life*!' replied the other girl enthusiastically. I was quietly horrified at the idea of blowing that much cash each week on rent. I was still dedicated to my mission of being a property owner. I had pictures of potential flats up on my vision board (also a picture of a pole) and a scrawled-out formula for happiness:

House + Loving Relationship + Satisfying Career = ☺

I was pretty sure $400 a week would more than cover a mortgage repayment on a modest apartment in outer Sydney. With my sights set on a mortgage (and paying it off as quickly as possible), I settled into life at The Club. Three to four shifts per week was 'full time' – anymore than that and you ran the risk of 'burning out'.

I had finished school (and turned 18) by now, passing with top marks that secured me a space in a Public Relations degree at a sought-after university. My insomnia was made worse by my erratic sleep habits, getting home from work at 4 a.m. then getting up again at 7 a.m. to get to University. Then sleeping the whole next day to 'catch up'. I got to know the girls and the regulars of The Club. Club regulars are, of course, not to be confused with your primary source of income: '*Your Regulars*'.

Chapter 3

My Regulars

I am 18 years old.

I loved my Regulars: men who'd book me for a few hours each week. Apart from feeling more comfortable hanging out with someone who was practically a friend, it made more sense financially to stay in the Private rooms for hours with one customer, rather than having to work the floor to bring in customers who'd only stay for fifteen minutes. A stripper is very similar to a salesperson; the product you're selling is yourself. Like in any sales role, you need to believe in the product, establish a connection, build rapport and trust, then close.

Closing was key. We didn't get an hourly wage, so time was money – if you weren't performing onstage, you were working the floor, hustling. I spent no more than ten minutes with a customer (unless they were particularly witty or charming), before slipping my offer of a dance into the conversation – 'Do you want to see my office?'; or 'Do you want to see me naked?'; or my personal favorite: 'What's a nice guy like you doing in a place like this?'

I worked with an Eastern European woman named 'Destiny' (So many customers asked if that was her real name. C'mon guys!), who took a different approach. She simply leant on the customer's table, locking their eyes in her steely gaze and in her husky voice, asked, 'Vont show?' I'm not sure if it was intimidation, domination or genuine desire, but I can't quite believe the amount of times this worked – Destiny was always busy. Being a non-exotic Aussie girl, I stuck with my 'friendly girl-next-door' approach: 'You know, what you're saying is *really* interesting, I would loooooove to keep talking to you. In fact, we should continue this conversation … in a Private room out back.'

Some nights were simply magical – money attracts money, and once the cash started flowing I got caught up in its golden glow. I felt radiant as I swanned through the club, Privates booked back-to-back, with up to an hour's wait for eager customers to have a show with me. Men in strip clubs get caught up in pack mentality: 'Everyone seems to want a dance with this girl. I want to have a dance with her, too!' I drank champagne and danced, and collected my wad of fifties and hundreds at the end of my shift.

Some nights were the exact opposite. Stripping is not a job where you can hide your bad day behind a computer screen. You can't have personal or relationship issues. (Relationship? What relationship? Strippers are *always* single). You can't be sick, ever – I once did an entire Private Show with my head tipped back so snot wouldn't pour out of my running nose.

You most certainly do not get your period.

I remember asking a busy change room what the girls all did the week they were bleeding.

'I don't roster on.'

'If it happens at work, I go home.'

'I leave my tampon in as long as possible. Let the smell percolate. The guys love it.'

'Sea sponges. They're also great if you want to have sex with your period and don't want your guy to know.'

'Sea sponges?! But how do you get them out?'

'Yeah … that can be tricky. Especially if they get stuck up in the back corner.'

'Does your uterus have corners?'

I would wear a black dress with black lingerie. I'd borrow a lighter to burn the string off my tampon and made sure I changed it every hour. On the hour. No way was I taking days off earning if I wasn't genuinely sick. There's no holiday or sick pay when you're a stripper. I was acutely aware that I couldn't do this forever. And I had an apartment to save for.

Customers knew none of this, of course. They came in to party and relax – our job was to sell them that fantasy, be their good-time party girls who laughed at their jokes, complimented them and treated them like kings. I taught myself to remember people's names. Once I scored a show because a man walked in the door and straightaway I called out, 'Hey Paul.' He looked shocked then delighted – it had been more than a month since his last visit. He walked me straight into a Private Show.

Other girls would pin up business cards to the noticeboard in the change room they'd collected from customers, often writing insults like 'Dickhead' or, even worse, 'Cheapskate' on them. Not me. I jotted a few key points on the back – 'three kids, loves surfing and having sex in public' – kept a kind of Rolodex of my Regular and Semi-Regular customers. I enjoyed fact-finding, going that extra mile to learn and remember their personal info. Although initially, I loved the fact that my earnings weren't dictated by my looks, but rather by my intelligence and wit, it slowly dawned on me (and you've probably figured this out already) that you don't actually need to be super-smart to be a stripper. Girls less intelligent than me, fitter than me, skinnier than me, fatter than me, prettier than me, or uglier than me could all make good money in the world of The Club. Stripping is a great equaliser. No matter what you look like, or who you are, to someone out there you are the 'perfect woman'.

You just have to hope like hell he comes in on a night you're rostered on.

A customer with a thing for pale redheads is going to book me over a buxom blonde every time. However, exceptions happen. One customer booked me for a show, spent the entire fifteen minutes telling me how he loved natural breasts more than anything, then booked Jasmine (with her surgically enhanced DDs) straight afterwards. I had to learn to accept that I wasn't going to be everyone's cup of tea – and, although I could pretend to be the shot-drinking, loud, boisterous party girl with groups of young guys out on a Buck's Night, it was tiring. I much preferred to spend my time with older businessmen. Them in their suit and tie, and me lying naked on my sheepskin rug, sipping champagne and discussing management styles and investment strategies.

There were days where I found customer after customer who was my 'type' and I'd leave work happy, slightly tipsy and very much 'in the black' financially.

Then there were days where nothing went right – my bra wouldn't come undone or I forgot to cut off my tampon string. Embarrassing moments like these were bad, but nights of not making money were the absolute worst. 'Another day, another dollar' is a terrible maxim when you have to take your pants off to earn that dollar. It made you completely second guess whether you should be doing the job in the first place. The industry self-regulates in that way – if you're not good at it then you're not making money, and if you're not making money you're going to seek employment elsewhere.

Usually somewhere that will let you keep your pants on.

I continued to fake it until I made it. I learned how to imitate the glow of a good night as best I could, strutting around the club with as much confidence as I could muster, although after four or five rejections in a row it was hard not to take it personally – when you asked, 'Do you want to see me naked?' the answer was an outright 'No.' When this happened, I would take some time out, have a drink, change my outfit ('it's this dress; it's definitely not me!'), or hang with the Bar Flies, who could always be counted on for a sympathetic ear, a drink – or sometimes a box of chocolates.

I made it a policy never to pay for my own drinks at work. I was there to earn money, not spend it. Many girls handed back a large chunk of their pay at the end of a shift to cover their expensive bar tabs. Not me. Customers always paid for my drinks. Towards the end of my time as a table dancer – when a drink had become essential to me being able to function in The Club – I'd go in for a sale and, if I failed to close, I'd say, 'Well, the penalty for not having a Private Show with me is buying me a drink.' And voilà! A glass of champagne with a bright red strawberry impaled on the rim found its way onto the table.

Those were heady days for a teenage girl. I was given lingerie, perfume, chocolates, flowers and poems. I formed a kind of relationship with my Regulars. Spending several hours together every couple of weeks, sharing drinks and a meal (The Club had a restaurant), meant I got to know intimate details about their lives and shared an edited version of my own. Working as a stripper is a chance to create whatever life you want for yourself. One girl took this to the extreme, telling people she was raised by a tribe in the Amazon jungle. I went through a phase of telling different tales to different people (even adopting an English accent for one whole shift), which was fine, until some of these same people reappeared in the club and wanted to book me again. I couldn't remember what I'd told to whom and felt very sheepish when someone asked, 'Weren't you English last time?'

Eventually I developed a bio and background for Suzie that was similar to mine, and I stuck with the one story so it was easy to remember. Suzie lived in a suburb near me. She was studying Public Relations, but at a different University. She was single (of course). She loved her body. She was 'small, cute and bouncy' and was always having FUN! She even had a 'real' name that she would disclose to *very* special customers – 'Amy'. Suzie/Amy was still Emma, but she was the distilled elements of my personality. It was like I put Emma inside a centrifuge. The loud, confident parts that spun out became Suzie and anything shy, gentle or soft was buried deep down inside. I used to visualise myself flicking on the 'Suzie Switch' at the start of a shift. Even later in my career, when I was teaching a pole class, emcee-ing a large event or even just being around a lot of people I didn't know very well, I still found myself doing the same thing – it felt safer to interact with people as Suzie, rather than as Emma.

It was a delicate balancing act. You had to share parts of yourself with strangers without really sharing anything at all. You had to spin the illusion of availability. The possibility that maybe, just maybe, they might have a chance with you is what kept customers coming back. But if they fell for you, you were toying with someone's emotions. I never felt comfortable about that. One customer loved *scungies* (the sports knickers you wear in primary school under your sports skirt). He bought me a pair each week and booked me for an hour to model them. He kept pushing for a date and, when I told him it wouldn't happen, he cried. I felt heartless and mercenary.

A long-haired hippie named Tom often came in and played pool with me. On learning about my penchant for all things pink and girly, he'd arrive bearing gifts of My Little Ponies and Barbie Dolls. On the odd occasion we went for a Private, he never wanted to see me naked. We usually played pick-up sticks with matches we stole from the bar.

Not getting naked actually happens more often than you would think – some guys really only want to talk and hang out. I think they were paying for the outrageousness of our stripper selves. Normal girls don't act like strippers and strippers don't act like normal girls. Just like Jasmine clutching at the gun holster of the cop, Suzie did things that Emma would never have dreamed of – such as body shots off the other girls, 'accidentally' dropping the pool cue and hoisting her skirt up a little higher before bending over to pick it up. Flashing her boobs to distract a customer just as he was trying to sink the black. It was stupid and it was fun. The attention from customers was gratifying and the tips accompanying that admiration justified my actions as 'part of the job'.

Tom and I actually became friends. Eventually we shifted our games of pool from The Club to the local pub. And that was the thing; I actually struck up friendships with some of these men, some of which lasted for years – I cared about them and they cared about me. When I first started learning pole tricks, my inner thighs were speckled with blue and purple bruises from forcing my soft skin to contort around a metal tube. A customer pulled me aside after our show and, brimming with anxiety, asked, 'Is someone, like … *hurting* you?' I laughed and reassured him it was from trying to flip myself upside down. But I couldn't help but feel touched by his concern for a girl he barely knew.

I had a lovely older Regular client, who would book me for fifteen minutes but only ever wanted to see me topless – which he had just seen out on the main stage. He was very old-fashioned and felt that nudity was going just a bit too far. He wore hand-knitted sweaters and thick horn-rimmed glasses. He was tall and gangly, with loose folds of skin around his neck and a balding scalp. He still sends me a birthday card each year with $20 inside to buy myself 'something nice'.

Another customer had a thing for watching girls getting changed. I slipped out of my stripping get-up and into my track pants or jeans, then out of my track pants and back into my lycra evening wear. Stripping out of 'normal' clothes is extremely challenging. Stripping clothes are designed for stripping. The fabrics are stretchy so you can shimmy out of them, the bras either have ties or clips (a normal bra clasp can secure itself closed if you lie on your back on a hard stage) and the G-strings have clips on the sides so you don't get them caught around your six-inch stiletto-heel. There's nothing worse than a stripper who can't get out of her clothes.

Without fail, my track pants got caught around my foot and I ended up doing an awkward little hop around the tiny stage in the Private room, before giving up and taking them off lying down. I could make it through about four or five changes during my fifteen-minute show, always timing it so I was back in my evening wear, ready to find my next customer without a moment's pause, at the end of our show. Club Rules were that you had to be in full (sexy) evening wear while working the floor and your dress had to fall two inches below your knee. It could be completely see-through, as long as it was below your knees. It was almost like being back at my Private school – girls would be sent home from The Club if their dresses were too short.

Another customer thought it was hilarious to bribe the DJ to play 'Suzie Q', by Creedence Clearwater Revival, whenever I was performing on the main stage.

I hated it.

Luckily, that same customer also tipped me $50, which helped me hate it a little bit less. The way I felt about the song that was playing while I danced had a direct impact on my earnings (and therefore a direct impact on my apartment fund). I loved performing and, if I loved the song and really got into it, I did a better show, which meant more money. If people can see you're enjoying yourself onstage, they enjoy it, too. Some of those 'into it' podiums were spectacular, tipping dollars being thrown by the handful onto the stage, while I flew around the poles. I would flash a beaming smile and make eye contact with each customer in the room, they would smile back. There was no malice. It was almost as if I was inviting them into the dance with me. My joy became his joy. It didn't matter who he was. Young, old, Asian, Indian, Australian, European. For a moment he too could experience the magic spell I was weaving. I was completely at home and comfortable – and as I invited him in with my smile, I shared my golden glow with him and he felt that way too.

After a few weeks of 'Suzie Q' podiums, the DJ began to announce me as 'Suzie Q' and, gradually, the other DJs and staff followed suit.

I began to feel my real self slipping further and further away. 'Emma' began to sound more and more foreign to me. I began to feel suspicious when people called, asking after what I referred to as 'the E-word'. My voicemail message changed from 'Emma' to 'You have reached one small redhead' and, finally, to 'Suzie Q' – which it still is today.

Another Regular would book me and my school-friend (who was now working at The Club with me). He must have had some kind of change-room fantasy, because his request was to ignore him completely and undress each other, all the while bitching about the popular girls from school, wondering what they were doing right now. I would absently help her out of her bra and knickers and say, 'Or what about Vivian? I bet she's married with three kids by now.' I'm not sure what he got out of this, but we took it as a great opportunity to catch up.

Yet another would book me for two shows (half an hour). He wanted me to stand naked on the podium with my hands on hips facing him (not moving, not talking; just standing), for the first fifteen minutes. Then, at the halfway mark, he would ask me to turn my back to him and continue standing with my hands on my hips, presumably so he could bask in my rear view. Foot fetishists didn't even glance at the rest of me, just stared in rapture at my toes for the full fifteen minutes!

My goal was an apartment, so I was happy to acquiesce to these 'unusual' requests that some of the other girls turned their noses up at. As long as my customers were happy and kept coming back for more, I didn't mind doing things that were a bit unusual. And if a customer asked me to do something I was uncomfortable with – like talking dirty to him – I knew that, ultimately, I was a naked woman. And therefore I had all the power.

'Do you think my areolas are different sizes?' I asked, bunching up my boobs to create a killer cleavage and pulling the two nipples closer together for easier comparison. Distraction was the key. Being asked to do things I was uncomfortable with, and being strong by not doing them, slowly helped reveal to me where my boundaries were. I think anyone who works in the sex industry has to know and respect their own boundaries – porn stars, for example, are able to have sex on camera in a room with a few people present, but may be uncomfortable getting naked in front of hundreds of people. For me, my sexuality was so on display that my actual sex life was something I wanted to keep quite private and personal. However, like my body and mind, I toyed with the idea that my sexuality was a commodity that could be traded for cash. It was a very special customer, we'll call him 'Richard', who made me question just which parts of me were and weren't for sale.

Rich Dad, Poor Dad, Sugar Dad(dy)

I am 18 years old.

He was sitting in the Diamond Room at a table with another, much older, man. The two of them were deeply engrossed in conversation, ignoring me and (more frustratingly) the large pile of dancer dollars in front of them. I rolled around seductively on my 'Pussy Pelt' – a sheepskin rug I toted around the club to protect my pale skin from the inevitable bruises that cropped up on my knees from crawling on hard podiums. Also for hygiene reasons – I was sliding my naked ass around a podium that had the asses of about thirty other girls sliding around on it each night. The men were both wearing tailored suits and expensive watches that, coupled with the fact they were in the Diamond Room, meant they had some money to burn.

'Excuse me, you may not have noticed but I'm naked here.'

He slowly turned away from his companion and looked me up and down. I would say he undressed me with his eyes, but it went further than that (besides, I was stark naked). It was almost as though he saw the Emma behind Suzie. He spoke slowly, in a measured, even tone with no hint of emotion.

'Excuse me, we're talking here.'

At first I was taken aback, then indignant – *Nobody speaks to me like that!* I was used to being treasured like a little princess. I persevered, determined to not only win him over, but also to coax him into a Private.

'Yes, but I'm naked.' I jiggled my breasts a little to emphasise my point.

'Hi Naked, I'm Richard.' He offered his hand for me to shake.

'There's a fine for Dad jokes.' I ignored his outstretched hand and pointed at the pile of dancer dollars. Made of laminated plastic, customers had to purchase dancer dollars from reception (so the club could take a cut). They were valued at two dollars each and came in bundles of five. Richard picked up five bundles ($50 worth) and slid them into my garter, sliding his hand down my leg as he moved it away. He was wearing a crisp white shirt with silver cufflinks. He practically reeked of money. He introduced his companion as his father. *Interesting choice of strip-club buddy*, I thought.

'Hi, I'm Suzie,' I said, eager to regain control of the situation. 'What do you do?'

'I work in insurance.'

'For one of the big companies?' I was trying to gauge his salary and how much play money he might have to blow on strippers.

'No. I own my own brokerage firm.'

A lot. He had a lot of play money.

After some banter back and forth, eventually, I convinced Richard to take me for a Private Show.

Throughout the whole fifteen minutes, he kept reiterating that he was 'bored', that this was 'doing nothing for me', and could he please call me to take me out on a real date. This is a pretty standard line (not the 'doing nothing for me' – I hadn't actually been told that before, but strippers decline date requests from customers on a daily basis).

'I don't have a phone,' was my standard response when asked for my number. (This line sometimes resulted in an unexpected gift; I was given no less than three phones over the course of my stripping career.) With Richard I demurred with …

'I don't know you well enough to see you outside of here; perhaps, if you took me for a few more shows, we could get to know each other a bit better?'

He said he'd be back the next day to see me again.

I couldn't stop thinking about him that night. He was funny and smart, and there was something about him that felt different from the other men who had tried to prise me free of the safety net of The Club. During my shift the next day, I kept looking hopefully at the entrance, wondering if he would show. To keep my mind occupied, I threw myself into the day's earnings. There is a general financial rule of thumb that says you should try and live on 70 per cent of your income and save the remaining 30 per cent. I took this in inverse proportions

– I was determined to live on 30 per cent of my income and increase my income as much as possible. I only ever spent what was left after saving. Not the other way around. Every day had its own balance sheet – if I worked at The Club (earning $400) and spent $6 on my train ticket and $7 on a sandwich after work, net profit: $387.

I set my own sales targets; I would try to do a minimum of one fifteen-minute Private Show for every hour I worked (usually a seven-hour shift). I periodically checked in with the receptionist throughout my shift to see how my earnings were going. Once I hit $300, it was an 'okay' day and, once I got more than $500, it became a 'good' day.

I'd just walked out of a Private that tipped my earnings over into an 'okay' day, when I noticed the back of Richard's tanned neck; he was sitting at a table away from the stage. My heart started thumping. I broke into a grin and trotted up to him.

'You came back!'

'You seem surprised?'

'Men sometimes lie.'

'And strippers don't?'

'No. Never.' I shook my head emphatically.

His handsome face broke into a grin. 'Liar.'

I took him by the hand and led him up to reception to book in for a Private. Once in the room, he told me not to bother taking my clothes off, he just wanted to get to know me.

He came in five more times to see me over the next couple of weeks and kept asking me to see him outside of the club. I was attracted to him, but unsure because of our age difference. He never told me exactly how old he was, but I guessed somewhere in his mid-forties. He asked me one more time to see me out of work and could he please have my phone number. I finally relented, gave him my number and I said I'd think about the possibility of a real date.

As my luck would have it, I happened to meet another customer called Richard at around the same time. This Richard owned a Public Relations firm and was looking for a PA. I was partway through my degree at this point and this seemed like a perfect internship and introduction to the industry. I gave him my number and he said he would call me in the next couple of days.

I was standing in my room, folding washing wearing a spiked collar, latex bra and knee-high PVC boots (practising), when the phone rang.

'Hi, it's Richard.'

I immediately assumed it was PR Richard. I made some inane small talk about the weather before switching into business mode, demanding a 'trial period' to see if things would work out between us. He said that was a good idea and agreed to meet me the next day in a café in the CBD. We agreed on a time and ended the call. As I hung up the phone, I suddenly had a weird sinking feeling in the pit of my stomach.

That was PR Richard, right? It had sounded like him…

Sort of …

Uh-oh …

Who had I just been speaking to?

I called Lynda. I told her that I had the feeling I might have 'accidentally' got myself into a trial relationship with some kind of multi-millionaire. I caught the train into the city the next day and, on the way, I kept replaying the conversation over and over in my head, trying to recall the exact timbre of his voice. *Surely it was PR Richard? It must have been.* I kept repeating this to myself as the train clacked its way into the city. I think, deep down, I knew it was not. That sexy, gravelly undertone was unmistakeable. Even as I approached the café, I was thinking, *Maybe? Maybe?* My heart was pounding in time with my high heels tapping on the pavement. A well-dressed man in a suit was standing outside our designated meeting site, his back to me.

He turned around.

It was *not* PR Richard.

I shrugged internally. *You only live once; let's see where this goes.*

He took me by the hand and said he had rented a hotel suite for us. My mind whirled. *This was all happening too fast.* I took note of the address and room number, and texted it to Lynda – keeping one eye on the door the whole time. Looking back, this seems a little stupid and reckless; meeting a man I didn't know at all in a place I'd never been to. At the time, I think I was caught up in my *Pretty Woman* fantasy. He spread out a picnic on the floor for us to share then he kissed me and said he would like to make love to me.

I had only slept with one other person at this point. I knew I did not want to have sex with this man right now.

I didn't even have lingerie on – I had been expecting a PR interview and was wearing cotton-tail knickers and the same business suit I had worn for my interview at The Club. I used the same line I'd used on him at work – that I didn't know him well enough and wanted to spend some more time together. To my utter amazement, he didn't push the point at all. He smiled, said 'that's probably a good idea' and that after we had eaten he would like to buy me something. Assuming jewellery or lingerie, I was quite taken aback when he marched me down the road into a bookstore.

We went straight to the Business section where he starting pulling books off the shelf, piling them into my arms. He bought me the entire *Rich Dad, Poor Dad* series. Depositing the bag into my arms outside the store, he told me I'd need to have the first book finished and be ready to discuss it at our lunch date the following week. I stood blinking in the sunshine, wondering what the hell I was getting myself into but determined to go along for the ride.

Ever the over-achiever, I read all five books before meeting Richard the next week at a little French restaurant in Sydney. He spoke fluent French, Italian, Arabic and a host of other languages. Whenever we hopped into a taxi, he was almost always able to converse with the driver in their native tongue. He told the driver I was a visiting model from Paris, and I mombled in my schoolgirl French, mostly saying 'Oui, oui,' to answer his rapid-fire French. He loved creating little dramatic vignettes whenever we were out.

At our weekly luncheons, he taught me about leveraging equity in real estate. He shared the details and figures of the property investment deals he was working on – he was an insurance broker but dabbled in other investments and projects. I learned about Returns on Investment (ROI) and about positive, negative and neutral gearing on investment properties. Our table would be littered with napkins and pieces of paper, with figures and calculations scrawled all over them. He talked to me about my inner energy field – making me hold out my hands to feel the sensations between my palms, then move them closer together and further apart. He held a fork in his hands, rubbing it with his thumbs until it became hot to the touch, before twisting it into some kind of fantastical shape.

'How did you do that?' I asked.

'Energy,' he replied.

This had been going on for a few weeks when I realised that, pretty soon, he was going to want to escalate things on a physical level. I thought about it carefully. I realised I actually wanted to continue seeing him. Although I wasn't in love with him, I cared about him and thoroughly enjoyed spending time with him. The first time we slept together was at a Novotel. We'd just been to a beautiful restaurant for lunch and I was feeling thoroughly wined and dined. Probably a little too much wine on my part, but I was nervous. Turned out I needn't have been. The sex was good and we began to add the odd hotel visit after some of our boozy lunches.

I was finally living out my *Pretty Woman* fantasy, with

my very own 'Richard Gere'. He once snuck me into the men's toilets at Forty One, a five-star restaurant, so I could see the glass urinal where men could feel like they were pissing all over the city. Every few weeks, I was flown Business Class to join him around the country. We ate at incredible restaurants, spent time in the 'high-rollers' section of casinos and slept together in the suites of amazing five-star hotels.

I tossed and turned at night, fighting my insomnia. He told me I had control – 'Yes, yes,' I said, thinking I knew it all. 'Mind over body.'

'No,' he said sombrely … 'Mind over mind.'

I had no idea what he was talking about and stared at him jealously as he nodded off within a few minutes of lying down. I often got up, padding quietly to the window and looked out at the cityscape of wherever we were. The lights of the city shone out of the darkness and I wondered if people could see me, peering out between the curtains. Richard usually sensed when I was gone and, within about twenty minutes, came and gathered me into his arms, and ushered me back into bed.

I truly cared for Richard and he did for me as well, but I wasn't ever going to be in love with him. Our relationship continued for several years. Apart from teaching me about property investment, he also insisted I get a 'respectable' job – he was concerned about the growing gap on my resume while I was working at The Club. I managed to land an Office Manager's role in the PR department of a major religious institution; to this day, I have no idea how I got hired. Richard had taken me out for a wine-filled lunch before my interview and I remember gasping naked in the bathroom of an inner-city serviced apartment, while he sprayed me with cold water from the shower nozzle, force-feeding me black coffee in a last-ditch effort to sober me up before meeting my prospective employer.

'Can't get more respectable than that!' I yelled triumphantly at him, when they called to offer me the position. I think he was quietly impressed with how far I had taken his suggestion, although, I knew he sometimes worried about his influence over me.

'I've spoiled you. I've given you a taste of this life now – the hotels, the food, the shopping.'

'Not a problem,' I replied. 'I'll be able to afford it for myself one day.'

Being with him, and experiencing his luxury lifestyle, had sparked up my ambitious streak. I no longer wanted just my own apartment. I wanted several apartments.

I wanted to be a millionaire and retire by the age of thirty.

Saving the money I earned from stripping seemed like the fastest, easiest and most fun way to achieve this. Richard disagreed; he felt that, between his gifts and my office job, I should have enough money to stop stripping.

'Giving up stripping is easy,' I laughed, 'It's giving up the money that's hard.'

The truth was, I loved the underground world of The Club. I felt like I was part of this secret society, with its own dress code, rules and language. I had my friends, my rituals and my role models – the Showgirls.

Chapter 5

Feminist Stripper?

I am 19 years old.

'I'd like to take you for a Private Show.'

'Yes! I would love that; I definitely want to get naked for you. Can we just wait fifteen more minutes, though? I really need to watch this girl dance.'

I took the bemused customer by the hand and led him towards the main stage, where we both sat front and center to watch Bobbi – my favorite Feature Showgirl. My mouth hung open in awe and wonder and, at the end of her show, I clapped and cheered louder than any of the customers.

Feature Showgirls were special guest strippers, who would come in to do a single fifteen-minute show on the club's main stage. They had spectacular themed costumes – bringing to life all the typical male fantasies (nurses, cowgirls, dominatrices, cops, Las Vegas showgirls, pussy cats) – covered in diamantes and sparkles, with discreet zips and clips for ease of removal. The most exciting part was that they could choose their own music to dance to (no Creedence Clearwater Revival for them). Bobbi's pole skills blew my mind. Her long tanned limbs sailed around the metal tube like gravity didn't exist. Every movement was graceful and her stage presence was completely captivating. I desperately wanted some of her magic to rub off on me – I wanted to be even half as good as she was. She was like a stripper princess.

I took any opportunity to be near her and talk to her. I collected the discarded pieces of costume she'd stripped off during her show – always left in a neat pile in the center of the stage, well out of reach of any customers salivating for a 'souvenir' – and trundled into the change room after her, my arms laden with corsetry and PVC, dripping with sweat and sequins. Panting and sipping water, her perfectly moulded body glistening like a racehorse, she and I would do a roll call …

'Bra and G-string?'

'Yup.'

'Corset, chaps and hat?'

'Yup, yup, yup.'

'Hot pants?'

'Here you go.'

I fingered each item longingly as I handed them back, relishing these few seconds alone with her. 'Great show,' I mombled and she smiled back at me. She was tall and thin with natural breasts – an anomaly among 'Career Strippers' – and golden brown hair falling past her waist. When the DJ introduced her as the 'Australian Showgirl of the Year', I marvelled. This was the first time it occurred to me that there were competitions for this kind of thing. For stripping. The concept of being a Feature

Showgirl began to appeal to me – I loved performing and being the center of attention onstage. Plus, you were paid a show fee on top of what you earned through your Privates and podiums.

If you want something, all you have to do is ask. I approached management and performed my first Feature about a week later to a Britney Spears medley. I didn't have a fancy costume so I wore my actual old school uniform. I tied my white button-up shirt around my waist and used Mom's sewing scissors to hack my grey pleated skirt so short that it almost revealed the bottom of my butt cheeks when I was standing up (and most definitely did when I bent over). Wearing my school tie, with my hair in pigtails, the look was complete. I was the living, breathing embodiment of 'Private Schoolgirl Fantasy'.

Why do men have such romantic notions about schoolgirls? Some may say inappropriate notions, but perhaps they're simply reliving the lost days of their youth? Perhaps they failed to admire the tartan-clad nymphs around them during their awkward teenage years – too preoccupied with their acne, voice changes and unbidden erections, so now was their opportunity to truly appreciate that which they had missed. Being only freshly out of school myself, it didn't feel that weird. I had, after all, been wearing my 'costume' for real only a few months previously. I think a strip club is controlled and safe environment, where customers can indulge in these kinds of fantasies, customers can flirt and admire naked girls without technically 'cheating' on their partners. The vast majority of customers are there to worship the naked goddesses undulating around the poles and on the stage. Of course, the odd guy is on a mission to make you feel as small as possible. But, overall, these men are not predators, they are not sick or twisted or depraved, they just want to be treated like a king, to have pretty girls fawn over them, admire them, laugh at their jokes and writhe naked in a sexy way. It's not real. It's a fantasy.

I was paid to play the part of a Goddess.

Outside the controlled environment of The Club, I never felt quite as safe. I certainly never proudly displayed my sexuality or my naked body. I needed to cover up and I did – becoming almost asexual in my track pants and baggy jumpers. Out on the street, there were no worshipful customers, no security guards to protect me. Walking home from work or uni was when I got catcalled and negatively commented on. Walking the streets at night, on my way to or from The Club, I felt vulnerable. The men on the street didn't praise me. Instead, they made me feel small. Uncomfortable. They commented on my body. Shouted out what they'd like to do to my body.

I am not the golden goddess out here. I play the part of daggy, social misfit, using my resting bitch face and goth/punk clothing to keep people at a distance. Women who proudly display their sexuality (strippers, porn stars, sex workers) get put down by other women; they're blamed for men's violence against women.

Why not blame the men? Why not blame the actual perpetrators?

Inside The Club, there are security cameras throughout and in every Private room. Giant security guards patrol the Private rooms. The relationship between a stripper and her customer is always mutually consensual. Rather than merely looking at you as a 'sex object', most customers want to interact with the 'real' you – beyond your stripper persona. He wants to feel special, to feel that you're giving him some part of yourself no one else gets to see. That it's not purely transactional. He's seeking intimacy and connection. He wants to believe it's real. Even if he knows it's not.

Some girls refused to let people in, sticking steadfastly to their stripper 'character' and their simplistic 'I love sex and being tied up' type lines. I once overheard this: 'Yes, I'm attracted to women. When I catch a glimpse of my reflection in the mirror, I get turned on because I can see my breasts. Mmmmm … Look at them,' followed by a lascivious lick of her own nipple. I don't know what stunned me more – her audacity, or the fact that the customer in front of her was lapping it up, swallowing every word she said. I found it easier to stick to the truth (or my approximation of it) and be myself.

Well … be Suzie.

As strippers, we reinforce sexual stereotypes, but it's so very staged and obvious that the naiveté of customers who believed our ruse constantly surprised me. It was through stripping and nude modelling that I learned to be completely at home in my body. I've had every square inch of it examined and commented on and, although I was scrutinised onstage, I was also always hyper-aware of who was looking at me. My income depended on it.

My time onstage at The Club was my time to be on display. I would hum, 'How much is that doggie in the window?' under my breath on my way to do a podium. As I flashed my dazzling smile around the room, it was vitally important to note who smiled back, who was making eye contact, and who was staring most intently at my body. These were the men I'd make a beeline for as soon as I was offstage. They were a guaranteed Private Show.

In The Club, men had to pay for access to my body and mind. Once I was well into my stripping career, I remember growing increasingly frustrated when posing during a life modelling class. The artists kept asking personal questions like, 'What are you thinking about?' and 'What does your boyfriend think of you doing this?' I was already naked. They did not have the right to any other part of me, especially my personal stuff. In The Club, I expected and fielded the same questions, but the money I was paid soothed any annoyance I may have felt. However, this was an art class. The $20 an hour I was being paid did not buy my emotional labour.

...

Suzie Q became my armour. Private Show rejections no longer hurt – they weren't rejecting me, they were rejecting Suzie Q and Suzie Q wasn't a real person. She was hyper-feminine, almost like a parody of female sexuality. Applying my make-up for each table-dancing shift, it felt like putting on a mask. Smokey eyes, big glossy lips, fake eyelashes, hair perfectly coiffed, manicured, pedicured, buffed and golden brown (I had become quite adept at applying fake tan each week). I used to spend hours painstakingly plucking my bikini line – the frame for Pandora's box, which I was paid a small fortune to open for men to look inside (shaving left ingrown hairs and I couldn't let a full bush develop in between waxes). I liked feeling in control when I was looked at in a sexual way. I became almost deliberately 'unsexy' outside of work; I'd avoid make-up and sloth it in big cotton knickers and track pants (my legs remained unshaved whether at work or not). It gave me that same feeling as the first time watching Julia Roberts in *Pretty Woman*. Like I was getting away with something. I'm a grubby little university student but after thirty minutes in the change room … Voilà! … I'm an incredible sexual goddess. Even when Richard insisted I get acrylic nails and wear designer clothes, I didn't feel like myself. I felt like I was playing a role in a movie. A very glamorous and fun movie, but not quite 'me' – instead, I felt elated when he complimented me on a dress I'd bought from a second-hand shop.

Don't get me wrong – I loved my glamorous dresses, high heels and gorgeous lingerie. With my hair curled, my showgirl face on and sparkly jewellery, I could cast a spell over the whole club when I got up onstage. People watched, applauded and complimented me. But it was all fake. I'd walk past men from The Club out on the street, with my hair in a ponytail and my make-up wiped off, and the same guy who only days, or sometimes mere hours, before had been showering me with compliments and begging me to go out with him, barely deemed me worthy of a second glance. Lots of guys wanted to fuck Suzie Q. But very few wanted to get to know and date Emma. It made me shut Emma away even more. She needed to be protected from these men. They equated what they saw onstage with who I was as a person. They equated Suzie Q with Emma.

You can't reduce me, as a person, and my sexuality, to what you're seeing onstage. What you're seeing onstage isn't real. What *is* real is me, in my pyjamas, with a stuffed animal in one hand and cup of tea in the other. What's real is a seventeen-year-old girl, crying real tears of frustration as an entire room of her peers turns against her and genuinely believes that feminism destroyed the 'happy family'.

For me, feminism is the freedom for a woman to do whatever it is she wants to do —whether that's be a high-flying CEO, or raise three kids. Or do porn. Or be a sex worker.

Or all of the above.

And to do it without other people criticising her.

Men can do any, or all, of these things without anybody raising an eyebrow. We don't have to refer to this as 'Meninism'.

I say, people; what has been most hurtful is when I cop criticism from women.

Women who are trying to be 'taken seriously' in a patriarchal society see strippers as 'making it worse by replicating and perpetuating every stereotype we are trying to break down' (This is paraphrased from the editor of a magazine who once interviewed me for an article). This was a woman who, by her own admission, had never set foot in a strip club. And therein lies the problem. Most of the arguments and criticisms I've come up against are from people who have no first-hand experience of the industry they are denigrating. They get their ideas and arguments from the media or from movies (neither of which tend to put forward a positive image of female strippers). Imagine if the movie *Magic Mike* had been about female strippers? Girls taking drugs, having sex with strangers and taking their clothes off for money – would it have garnered such a cult following?

Yes, there is a strong power imbalance between men and women in society. But that is why I liked being a stripper. I had the power. I could stand naked, strong and beautiful, in my own sexuality and be admired for it – not only that, I could charge for it. This is not what most women experience. For many, if not most of us, overt sexual behavior is seen as an invitation to violence, particularly sexual violence. Because strippers give the illusion of being available and sexual, we are blamed for perpetuating this stereotype and power imbalance. However, there are very strict conditions around our availability and our sexuality. Yes, it is on display and it is available at certain times. Provided that certain safety conditions have been met. Also, there's a fee.

I'm going to be objectified and whistled at on the street, anyway. I may as well have some control over it, and get paid for it.

My concerns about my role in perpetuating power imbalances between men and women by being a stripper all changed one night, when I stumbled across an underground event called 'Gurlesque'. Held monthly in different venues, it was the forerunner of the city's now-thriving Burlesque scene. Gurlesque was founded by four queer performers, including two pierced and tattooed strippers deemed 'too alternative' for the Club X peep show where they were working. A peep show is not like a table-dancing club. The strippers are ensconced in a glass room and customers insert coins to roll a window up and reveal the girls for a few moments at a time. There is no interaction between girls and customers – the men are in their own private booths, watching the girls through a glass screen, often masturbating as they watch the girls writhe, tantalisingly out of reach.

Sex Intents and Glita Supernova were their stage names and Gurlesque was the ultimate celebration of the female body and female sexuality. Anyone could grace that stage – amateur, professional or anywhere in between. Your size, shape or age didn't matter. The night was for women and queers only, and showed the endless creative possibilities of erotic performance art when you remove the stereotypical notions of what constitutes 'sexy'. There were no rules. This sense of freedom made me feel that Gurlesque was what stripping could be … What stripping *should* be.

My first night there, I watched Elizabeth Burton who, at age 62, was one of the oldest showgirls. She was dressed in what can only be described as her 'Sunday

Best' – a fitted dress, hat and gloves – which I think my day job workmates would have totally approved of for church. Half of her show was a live tutorial: she spoke into a microphone while wielding a pair of sewing scissors, deftly snipping a pair of pantyhose into a (far sexier) garter belt and stockings.

She slipped into her newly created accessory then a rousing old-school striptease song blared through the speakers and she proceeded to strip out of them. She was the epitome of class – she held herself with elegant dignity – even when taking her bow stark naked at the end.

Lillian Starr played a gorgeous 1950s housewife, with an elaborate kitchen set-up onstage. She went through the motions of preparing and baking a pie, before a fire occurred in the oven and she stripped off her apron and dress (as you do when there's a fire) to the classic stripper track 'Cherry Pie', revealing a large strap-on dildo, with which she proceeded to fuck the freshly baked (you guessed it) cherry pie.

Nothing was sacred and nothing was off limits. It was pure entertainment. There were shows about menstruation, shows about poo, performers stripped as the prime minister, the US president, Eskimos and Lady Diana. Who knew stripping could be so innovative and political?! The whole concept blew my mind. I wondered how the male customers from The Club would react to this place. A woman – who was not dressed as a schoolgirl, nurse or Barbie-Doll Glamazon – was taking her clothes off? Unheard of!

Then Gayna Galaxy entered the stage. It was almost

as if a hush fell over the hitherto rowdy crowd. Gayna was the epitome of everything I ever wanted to be as a stripper. She was stunning, with a perfect body and pert fake boobs. But it wasn't just how she looked. She commanded attention – captivating the entire audience from the moment she stepped out. If Bobbi was the Stripper Princess, Gayna was the Queen. She hit every beat with a flick of her curly hair and occasionally paused to enjoy the effect she was having on the crowd, giving a wicked grin or a salacious wink. She oozed sex appeal, worked the audience into a complete frenzy and, afterwards, I was on my feet with the rest of the crowd in a standing ovation. A standing ovation? For a stripper?! I decided right there and then that I wanted to be a professional Showgirl. I wanted to be like Gayna. I wanted to *be* Gayna!

At the end of the show, I cornered Sex and Glita, and asked if I could please perform at next month's event. They were warm and welcoming. Their only guideline was to perform my 'own version of a strip show, whatever that might be – you can be topless, you can be naked, you don't have to take anything off if you don't want to.'

Complete creative freedom!

I was limited only by my own imagination, not someone else's prescription of what 'sexy' was. This was like a dream come true – a stripping utopia. I was part of the revolution! My first show there was called 'The Demise of Nikki Webster' (a famous Australian child star). I pranced around to her single 'Strawberry Kisses', before smothering myself in strawberry sauce, smearing the sauce and my make-up everywhere. At the end, I was a sticky mess with panda eyes and lipstick down to my chin. It was not perhaps typically 'sexy' but it was awesome.

I began to seek out regular bookings at Gurlesque and other 'queer friendly' performance nights. I performed a show as Marilyn Monroe, lap dancing a Director's chair, and another as a patient in a mental hospital, tied to a table with thick white elastic. I played Paris Hilton (getting more than a little friendly with a toy Chihuahua prop) and performed yet another show about thrush to Vitamin C's 'The Itch'. Yes, there was cottage cheese involved – prompting one of my friends to ask if there was anything I wouldn't do onstage.

'I don't insert,' was my reply.

I was subverting stripping and I loved it.

I loved taking my clothes off at these alternative stripping venues. No one tried to dictate what I should wear, how long my dress should be or what I should do in my shows – I loved the freedom.

I told Richard about the underground stripping scene, but he didn't get it. I'm not sure if any of The Club's clientele would have. Richard shook his head in a bemused way and warned me to be careful not to have any photographic or video footage captured of my performances.

'That stuff will come back to bite you,' he cautioned.

I did what he said, asking the professional videographer not to record my early shows – I still didn't know what I wanted to do with my life and I didn't want to jeopardise my future career.

I performed at the Hellfire Club, a Fetish/BDSM club night, where I was surrounded by people dressed in leather and harnesses, being tied up and spanked. I loved that I could do whatever the hell I wanted and could just have fun getting naked onstage. I performed as a Geisha and made nipple clamps out of chopsticks before doing an erotic 'tea ceremony' with UV paint under black lights.

I was booked at private BDSM parties – innocuous-looking town houses that, when you stepped inside, revealed dimly lit dungeons. These were lined with lustrous leather paddles and whips; an assortment of bamboo canes; every kind of restraint, cuff, gag or mask imaginable; and purpose-built harnesses, swings, cross beams and ornate wooden beds with black metal rings set at various heights in the four posts to secure willing or wayward submissives.

Medical rooms, with gleaming white tiles and harsh fluorescent overhead lights, were where dominant 'medical professionals' could carry out extensive and intimate examinations of their submissive 'patients'.

I sometimes stayed after my show, watching some of the play sessions going on around me with a sense of incredulous wonder. I got to know some of the people in the 'scene'. I have never before, or since, met a more open-minded and free-spirited group of people. At one party, I was dressed as a nurse and, as my outfit must have implied a certain level of medical knowledge, I was invited to assist with some nipple and genital piercings – holding lights and handing equipment to the professional piercer. I wasn't even twenty years old and it was so exciting to meet these underground groups of people, who were so open-minded and accepting. I felt like Suzie Q had hit her stride.

I took a booking to perform at a night called 'Hardcore Heaven'. The act before mine was beautiful. A ballerina danced *en pointe* to the theme from *Swan Lake*, slowly having her arms decorated with play piercings (ornamental and temporary small-gauge needles). Each needle was adorned with a black plume of feathers so, by the end of the show, she stood resplendent as the Black Swan, with small riverulets of red blood running from some of the needles.

I felt a little sick. Not from what I was seeing (although I'm not a big fan of needles), but because I was suddenly very, very worried that I was nowhere near 'hardcore' enough for this party. I felt inadequate and vanilla. They were going to hate me and boo me off the stage.

I sidled up to the organiser and whispered, 'Umm … I'm really sorry, but I don't know if I'm right for this event. I do not do anything remotely like that.'

'I'm sure whatever you do will be fine. They'll love it.'

Doubting her words, my abilities and also myself, I made my way onto the stage and nervously began my 'Ice Princess' routine, with a diamanté-encrusted costume, dry ice and body glitter.

Partway through my show, I realised in amazement she was right – they did love it! The crowd was incredibly appreciative. They were all yelling, clapping and cheering for more. There was no negative judgement from these people. No right. No wrong. Everything was okay. Everyone was welcomed and accepted, just as you were.

I couldn't help but compare this adoring, responsive crowd to the 'normal' strip clubs where I was doing Feature shows. One night, at a strip joint, I was dancing onstage to Nelly Furtado's 'Maneater' only to have a drunken guy in the front row (he may or may not have had all his teeth) yelling out '"Maneater", eh? What about a PUSSY EATER!' at random intervals throughout my *entire* show. I did what any professional would have done. Gritted my teeth and did my best to ignore him.

After that incident, I changed my playlist. Moving away from music tracks that pumped the crowd up into a maddening frenzy. I learned to dance to slow, mournful tunes with a sexy, resting bitch face. People don't shout obscenities at you when you're naked, have a soulful expression on your face and are slowly moving to 'Chasing Cars' by Snow Patrol, or 'Drops of Jupiter' by Train. They may not have appreciated the art form of what I was doing –the hundreds of dollars of costuming and hours of rehearsal that had gone into my show – but at least the audiences were respectfully silent.

At the very least, it stopped anyone shouting, 'take it off' at the top of their lungs.

I have never understood why people shout this at strippers. What else do they think I'm going to do? I still dream of one day stopping my show and shouting back, 'I don't come into your workplace and tell YOU how to do YOUR job.'

Maybe one day I will.

When I performed in regular strip clubs, customers seemed to forget I was a real person. That I go to the bathroom, eat breakfast and pay my bills, just like them. (Granted, I earned the money for my bills in a slightly different way to them.) They never considered how they would feel if someone said what they were saying to their sister or their girlfriend.

Or their daughter.

Well, they might think – *My sister or girlfriend would never do something like that.*

Are you sure? I am a sister. I am someone's daughter. I have worked with plenty of moms – for them stripping is a good option, especially with young kids. One colleague did pub shows on Friday afternoons and Feature Shows on Saturday nights so she could spend the weekdays with her toddler. I was working with her one afternoon at a pub venue. She pranced around the room as a cheerleader for her first song, shaking her breasts and pom poms, and wiggling her butt. She bent over in front of one patron to slide off her pleated skirt and he deliberately poured his entire beer over her while she was dancing. She somehow finished her show, but came backstage crying. We mopped her up as best we could with napkins from the bar. It made me feel sad; he had completely disregarded her realness.

How could someone do something like that?

Something about taking your pants off for a living seems to negate your right to respect.

I never copped even a hint of disrespect at 'alternative' stripping venues. And I think that was part of why I loved them so much. I was more than happy stripping at swingers' parties, where everyone was standing around wrapped in towels, at BDSM events like the Hellfire Club and anything that was for 'Girls Only. I felt at home and un-judged.

At one of these BDSM events, a man approached me after my show.

'I want to pay you to stand on me.'

'I'm sorry, what?'

'Stand on me.'

'Naked?'

'No.'

'What – like while you masturbate or something?'

'No. Just stand there. In jeans. I have a friend who will take some pictures.'

He confessed he had tried asking the girls at a local brothel to accept their normal fee, just to stand on him, and they had refused!

I was mystified at the girls' refusal. This sounded like easy money – and it was.

I met with the man, Matt, at his place with two other girls and, sure enough, just as he had said, we stood on him. Dressed in jeans. While his friend took photos. We even had tea and biscuits while we were doing it! Through Matt, I began to work at 'Trample Parties', where all manner of foot fetishists gather to be walked on. Chains hanging from the ceiling helped you balance and a sea of (clothed) male bodies stretched out beneath you. The added bonus was that someone was always willing to give you a foot massage afterwards.

Life back in the strip club seemed almost banal

compared to this glittering, perverted and exciting world I'd discovered. I began to wonder if this really would come back to bite me, as Richard had warned? After all – I wasn't using my real name, I didn't really look like myself and, dammit, I wanted some mementos. Something to look back on and say, 'That was me. I did that.' And so I began to get my shows videoed and photographed. Rather than something that could potentially impact a future career, I began to think of stripping *as* my career.

So now I was a career stripper. The over-achieving schoolgirl was still alive and well inside me; I decided I would be a high-achieving stripper.

A notice had been put up in the dressing room, inviting people to compete in a competition called 'Empress of Erotica'. As I was reading the rules, another girl walked in with a designer handbag held aloft – it was beautiful.

'Who wants this?' she announced. 'One of my regulars just gave it to me and if I take it home, my boyfriend will kill me.'

How stupid, I thought to myself. It was the first time this had occurred to me; the idea that a relationship could be incompatible with this job had never cropped up before. *I'd never date someone who was jealous like that*, I promised myself. *My boyfriend would be proud I'd scored a free handbag.*

I turned back to the notice and took one of the entry forms from the dressing-room bench. If I was going to compete, I was going to take it seriously, so I began to attend the weekly pole-dancing lessons that were held at the club. Part of my reason was also because Bobbi was the one teaching them. She came in on a Friday at

11 a.m. before the club opened at 12 p.m. to teach us pole tricks. I was there every time. I loved it. My background in gymnastics meant I took to being upside down quite naturally – and it gave my podiums an edge over the other girls.

I began to treat my podiums like a mini-feature show. I tipped the DJ to play songs that inspired me – songs I could really get into and enjoy dancing to. I loved the feeling of nailing an awesome podium. When the whole club would grind to halt to watch me dance. People not even bothering to put money in my garter – they'd simply throw fistfuls of dancer dollars onto the stage. Doing an awesome fifteen-minute podium that netted me around $200 also made financial sense – that was the same as doing four Privates. My apartment was getting closer.

I decided to step up and become a real Feature Showgirl. In order to attract higher fees for my shows, I needed some kind of title, so I entered 'Empress of Erotica'.

The winner would receive a sash, flowers, $1000 cash – and the all-important title. There would be three sections to the competition – an Evening Wear Parade (they provided a dress for this), a Swimwear Parade, for which we had to provide our own black bra and G-string ('swimwear' was interpretive, it seemed) – the rules specified it should be 'as erotic as possible' – culminating in a full nude twelve-minute show with 'no open legwork'. Different clubs and venues had different licensing laws. And although open legwork was de rigueur at The Club, it was not permitted at the competition venue. Any use of oils, creams and water had to be done on a floor covering or rug to avoid compromising the stage for the other dancers – you didn't want someone slipping over in your mess.

I was devastated to learn that the competition venue did not have a pole – all my practice had been for nothing. But, I was energetic and acrobatic. I used some of the 'tricks' learned from my shows at Hellfire (clothes pegs as nipple clamps and pouring candle wax over myself). I walked on my hands while naked and threw myself around the stage, before pouring body moisturiser between my breasts and between my legs. I came offstage with massive carpet burns on my knees and two blisters on my breasts where I had stubbed my candles out. I won the title of 'Best Breasts' (somewhat ironic, as I was the only one competing with natural breasts – and they were now blistered) and also 'Best Newcomer'. Best Newcomer is not really an award; it's more like a 'thanks for trying' or a 'participation' award. This was a wake-up call that I was a little out of my depth in the professional showgirl scene. Undeterred, I entered the very next competition that came up – the NSW State Heat for Miss Nude Australia.

If I thought I was out of my depth during Empress of Erotica, Miss Nude brought this home on a whole new level. These were proper career Showgirls, with thousands of dollars' worth of Swarovski crystals covering tailor-made costumes and incredible props; some of them even had stage assistants and back up dancers! I did a Lara Croft–inspired show, in some Bonds underwear that I had painstakingly sewed little elastic belt loops onto, in order to create an outfit worthy of raiding tombs. I had little plastic guns that I had spray-painted black on newspaper in the back yard. I flew up and down those poles, using every trick Bobbi had taught me. I won the title of 'Miss Petite' – pretty much the equivalent of 'Best Newcomer'.

However, a title was a title, and the fact that I now had two, coupled with being in the State final for Miss Nude Australia, still carried some weight. The owner of a striptease agency had seen my show; at the end of the night, she handed me her card. I called the very next day. By the end of that call, I was booked-out for the next six months, doing two to three pub shows per week. Pub shows, as the name implies, are strip shows performed in pubs. Some, like The Oxford Tavern in Petersham, were fully set up for strippers with a stage, pole, professional lighting and sound system. Others hired a DJ with portable speakers and placed a wooden cover over the pool table to create the 'stage'. The worst ones had no lighting, no stage and a little boom box that barely drowned out the sound of the customers talking. You were paid $120 for three, six-minute topless strip shows.

The pub scene was a showgirl's bread and butter. As a stripper, there was little else you could be doing at 3 p.m. on a Wednesday afternoon to earn come cash. The best part was hanging out backstage with the other dancers.

A couple of times, I was put on with Gayna Galaxy. To be in the same change room as her filled me with awe. We bonded while sewing sequins and diamantes back onto our costumes (we sometimes referred to the change room as the 'stitch-and-bitch zone'). She offered to help me out with some new costumes, as well as hair and make-up styling tips. I couldn't believe that I actually got to spend time with her, at her house! She had a dedicated 'costume room' with full-length mirrors, sewing machine, mannequins and endless tubs full of different-colored fabrics, sequins, trims, feathered headdresses, wings and costumes to suit any theme imaginable. I wondered if I would ever have a dedicated 'stripper room'. My costumes lived in a plastic crate under my bed. It was a Monday so we were both taking bookings and confirming shows for the week. She looked over at my diary. Every square inch was filled with scrawl, white-out and Post-It notes stuck over the top so I could fit more things in. Shifts at The Club, university lectures and tutorials, Rocky Horror on Fridays, two or three pub venues per week, three days per week at my PR office job, modelling gigs, plus all the other extraneous alternative bookings I did.

'Suzie,' she said seriously. 'You know, you need at least two full days off each week. In a row.'

I scoffed at her. *Who needs that?* I needed to earn money.

'When do you take time off?'

'When I'm sick or injured.'

She shook her head then taught me how to do proper Showgirl make-up and gave me some new eye shadows and costume pieces. She taught me that your 'arrival outfit' (what you wear to the venue) is just as important as your show costume. You should always show up to work with most of your make-up done, and looking classy and professional (no more track pants for me). I gave her some money, but she wouldn't accept anywhere near enough, simply telling me to 'pay it forward' to some other baby Showgirl someday.

I was just developing a name for myself around both the 'Alternative' and 'Normal' stripping scenes, when the worst-possible thing for my career happened.

I fell in love.

Chapter 6

I Lost Two Days

I am 20 years old.

Chris and I had gone to both primary and high school together. But I'd never looked at him in a romantic way. He had been the instigator and creator of my 'Poindexter' nickname at school. That and 'Surfboard' (my gymnastics-trained chest was 'flat with no fins').

Chris and I got drunk at a New Year's Eve party and ended up making out. He had to leave in the morning – I was still feeling fuzzy-headed and confused, but gave him my number when he asked for it. When he called, I had every intention of telling him I wasn't interested but, somehow, I found myself inviting him over. He ended up staying the night.

The next morning, he was running late for work. I have a pathological dislike for running late – ten minutes early is 'just on time' in my book. It's put me in good stead in the stripping industry.

'OMG, you're late! What can I do? What can I do?'

He stopped what he was doing, cupped my face in his hands and looked into my eyes.

'You can kiss me.'

It felt like time slowed down. His lips met mine and I lost myself, and my breath, for a few moments.

Chris was physical perfection – chiselled athletic body, strong jaw line and crystal clear blue eyes. He was intelligent, with a kind of wide-eyed innocence that was in stark contrast to the hard-nosed businessmen with whom I spent most of my time. Our dates consisted of movies, playing video games or eating fish and chips down by the harbour. We made up Elvish nicknames for each other and sent each other romantic notes, written entirely in the Elvish language created by Tolkien. For the first time in my life, I felt an amazing, all-encompassing, sense of love.

I took a great deal of pleasure in doing little romantic things for him – leaving notes on his car, or writing funny poems. The more time we spent together, the more I found myself thinking about him when we weren't together. My life became a weird hybrid of extreme kink mixed with the sweetness of new love. A diary entry from that time:

> Went to an open day at a BDSM parlour. Witnessed correct procedure for catheters and enemas performed on the house slave, known as 'Fuck Features', then met Chris for a picnic at Symphony in the Park. We shared cheese and biscuits and listened to the orchestra. It was lovely.

Chris seemed okay with my job at first. But from years of witnessing the experiences of the girls around me – most men are … at first. I kept the details of what happened each shift quite brief and told him boyfriends were banned from visiting their girlfriends at work, which was true. Knowing your girlfriend is a stripper is one thing; actually seeing it is an entirely different ballgame. Chris seemed to accept this. He'd meet me after work (around the corner of course) and I'd shout him dinner with that day's earnings. It almost felt like a way to 'make it up to him', after me flirting and being naked in front of other men all day.

At this point, Richard and I had been seeing each other for just over two years. If I was caught up in someone for a few weeks, Richard and I would sort of cool it, then pick back up again once I had moved on from whoever had been distracting me. I assumed things with Chris would be no different.

It was getting serious with Chris that ended my relationship with Richard.

To explain my frequent travel with Richard, I had told my family that I was working as a PA for an insurance broker, who sometimes needed me at interstate meetings. If they had looked in my small suitcase, they would have discovered lingerie, handcuffs and sex toys, rather than paperwork and a computer. I always had to check my luggage, no matter how small my bag was – no way my accessories would have made it on board as carry-on – although Richard always tried to get us to the airport late so I'd have to send the bag through the scanner. He grinned impishly at me, saying he couldn't decide who's face would be more hilarious – mine, or the poor airport security guard's.

On what turned out to be my last night with Richard,

I flew out to meet him. As the plane ascended, I gazed down at the twinkling lights, trying to pick out the house where Chris was at that moment. I cried softly to myself, wanting to be wrapped in his arms – not travelling to another city to have sex with someone else.

A limo collected me from the airport and took me to the hotel where Richard was waiting. I sat down on the bed and started crying.

He held me and asked what was wrong and, in between sniffles and choked sobs, I told him the whole story, how I hadn't expected to fall for someone, hadn't meant to … and yet, here I was.

'Are you in love with him?'

'Yes.'

He closed his eyes and nodded sagely. He said he understood completely, that he knew this would happen eventually. He even offered to pay for a separate hotel room for me for the night. I declined and stayed with him, but we didn't have sex.

When I returned, I felt lighter; I was free to be with the man I loved! I sat Chris down and explained the situation – what I had been doing, that there was no insurance company but that I'd ended it with Richard. I naively thought he'd understand and we'd live happily ever after.

He broke up with me.

I was devastated. I felt like I had lost a part of myself, like a limb. I felt like there was no point to my life without him in it. We only lasted a few days apart before he called me up and said he'd get back together with me, provided I told my parents about my stripping career.

I'm still not entirely sure what he hoped to achieve by this, but I was so desperate to be back with him that I went along with his idea. I even imagined (again, somewhat naively), that this would be a good thing and, perhaps, I could have an open and honest relationship with my parents, and not have to keep up the 'late-night waitress' charade any longer. I pulled Suzie out of the flattering strip-club lighting and into the harsh light of reality, by telling my mom first.

It did not go well.

'Mom, please sit down. I have something to tell you … I'm a stripper.'

'Oh my God, you're whoring yourself out on the streets to support your cocaine habit?'

'Umm … no, that's not what I said.'

Things didn't go any better with my dad. It put an awful strain on our relationship. He became quite distant from me for a couple of years. Our conversations, which had previously been filled with Daddy–Daughter love, became awkward. Stilted. I tried to talk about my job but he changed the subject. I tried to reassure him that I was safe and happy, but he reached as far away as possible from the topic – we discussed Lynda's boyfriend's part-time work, rather than how I earned money. It was gutting. This was such a big part of my life, my identity, who I was, and they were unable to accept it at all. I stand by my decision to tell them. I would rather have an honest relationship with my parents than one built on lies.

I realise it must be very hard for parents to come to terms with their baby girl doing things that they don't understand – and probably have no knowledge of, apart from what they've seen on the news and in films. Mom felt like she was condoning my decision to dance if I remained living under her roof.

One night, I was competing in a stripping competition called the 'Golden G-string' at The Oxford Tavern and, as I walked out the door, Mom called out, 'Off to degrade all women, are you?'

I moved in with Chris.

At first things were fine and happy, but then we began to fight. He hated what I did as a job. He hated the industry and he hated The Club.

'How can I ever respect what you do?' he asked me. I felt like he'd started seeing me as my job and not as a person. Like he didn't see me for who I was, rather as this one thing that I did. I am a human being. Stripping was a thing I did. It did not define me as a person. It was Suzie who was up onstage naked in a strip club, not Emma. He had access to Emma, the entirety of me – which no one else was privy to. But it still wasn't enough.

Things came to a head when he gave me an ultimatum: him or dancing.

I chose dancing.

I booked myself in for extra shifts at The Club. I even called one of my regulars, telling him I had just broken up with my boyfriend. He bought me a TV to cheer me up.

A few days later, Chris showed up at my office job and we fucked in the storage room. I think we were both slightly addicted to each other. God knows why else we would have hung on through all this. In a letter I wrote from this time:

> Chris apologised for asking me to choose between him and dancing. He said that he realised I had given up stuff for our relationship (namely going to BDSM parties and lesbian groups of friends … and I suppose Richard) … but it seems I'm clinging to dancing even more now. It feels so right for me and is such a huge part of me that for Chris to hate it so much feels a little bit like he doesn't love me – but rather someone else. Someone I am not.

We decided to start seeing each other again. But the fact is, I really don't like being told what I can and cannot do. The quickest way to get me to do something is to say I can't. The day he graduated from his course, I told him I'd meet him after work to celebrate. I took a day shift due to finish at 7 p.m., but a high roller came in and booked me and a group of girls for a show. He kept extending. And extending and extending. I stayed for the show, missing dinner entirely. It was 12 a.m. by the time I left work. The lure of the money was too much. I arrived at his house just after 1 a.m. Chris was sitting at his desk; the room was lit only by a small lamp on the floor.

'Have you been at work?' he asked, even though he knew full well where I had been.

'Yes. I am so sorry – but I did just make almost enough to pay this semester's uni fees in one night.'

He glared at me.

'Can I have a hug?' I asked tentatively. I wanted to feel his arms around me, to know that we were still okay.

'Not until you've showered. I don't want the stink of that place on you.'

I lowered my head and made my way down the hall to the bathroom. Desperate to do whatever he asked of me in order to make this right.

'And clean your teeth,' he called out after me.

Chris told me later that I had 'destroyed his self-esteem by choosing superficial relationships with other men over him.' I chose who I was, and what was important to me at the time, over him. I expected him to accept me for that.

I often prioritised work over relationships and friendships. I was on such a mission to earn money and succeed in the industry, I neglected important friendships – even skipping Lynda's 18th birthday because I had a shift at The Club.

Logistically, Friday and Saturday nights were my regular working week – unfortunately, they are the nights when most people socialise. My friends got sick of asking if I was free Friday or Saturday and, eventually, they just stopped asking altogether. This wasn't helped by the fact I'm also a bit of an introvert; work was a legitimate excuse to avoid social outings because I didn't want to be doing what most twenty-year-olds did on the weekend. 'Let's go out drinking and dancing' sounded exactly like what I did at work – it was the equivalent of me asking them to 'hang out at the office and file invoices.'

My social network began to be sourced more and more from work; people who kept the same hours as me, were keen for a movie or a quiet night at home, understood my workplace issues and, most importantly, did not make horrible comments about dancing. Who else would understand the hilarity of sticking your middle finger up at a customer, when he'd waved a $2 dancer dollar at you and asked, 'What are you going to do for this?'

When someone actually did that to me, I curled his hand back around the laminated plastic and said, 'I think you need it more than me.'

Strippers can't have bad days – not just at work, where it can affect your income, but you also don't have the ability to vent to your loved ones.

'I had an awful day at work today.'

From my non-work friends or family, the response was always the same. 'Well, why don't you quit, then?'

I learned I could only share 'happy' work stories with them. Stories that demonstrated how empowered I was, how much respect I was shown and how much fun I was having. The party-girl façade of work had to be maintained at home as well. It was exhausting. Every job has good days and bad days. No one else gets told to quit just because they had a bad day or met with a rude customer. Just like any other job, where you have to deal with the general public, there are nice guys and there are assholes. It's just worse in the The Club, because you're naked and the assholes are drunk.

So much for the honest and open communication I wished to have with my family.

Chris and I decided to have another go at our relationship, on the condition that I would no longer work in The Club. I'd only do pub shows, with no personal interaction or ongoing 'relationships'. This meant he was okay with me taking my clothes off, just not talking to someone while I was doing it. I had missed him so much that I agreed to his rules. I quit table dancing, I quit my part-time job and I went to work full-time as a debt collector for a group of schools. The tiny office felt like it was suffocating me. I had gone from champagne-sipping glamorous Goddess, basking in admiration and flattering stage lights, to basking in harsh fluorescent lighting in a windowless box.

I hated it.

From my diary at the time:

> I must really love my parents and ex-boyfriend because I have the distinct feeling that I took this job for them.

I had a horrible job, a relationship that was a long way from good, terrible rapport with my parents thanks to Chris's brilliant idea of telling them about Suzie, and was now isolated from my social networks as well. This put even more pressure on my relationship with Chris, as I expected him to fill all these gaps I now had in my life – being all things to me at all times. Which, of course, was impossible.

The net result …?

I was spiralling slowly into a black pit of depression. I went to see the doctor; straightaway, she gave me a prescription for anti-depressants. I began taking them, but failed to see an improvement. In trying to be what other people wanted me to be, I was losing who I really was.

My phone beeped one day with an intriguing text message – one of the high rollers from The Club wanted a group of girls to come perform at a five-star serviced apartment in the center of Sydney. The pay was $700 and it was unspecified what we were expected to do. Being a doting and obedient girlfriend, I asked Chris if I could go. He said no.

I went anyway.

I was running late because I'd been fighting with Chris that morning. I didn't even need to check the room number on my phone; I could hear screams of laughter and fits of giggles the moment I got out of the lift. I opened the door to a veritable cornucopia of excess. Five semi-naked girls were laughing and chatting. There was a huge pile of lingerie on the floor, generous platters of fruit and cheese, and free-flowing expensive champagne. Capped off with a breathtaking view through the floor-to-ceiling windows.

'Soooozzziiieee,' yelled a drunken John from underneath two girls, who were lap dancing him.

'Choose what you want to wear.' He gestured to the pile of satin-and-lace knickers and bras on the floor and I noticed, for the first time, they all still had tags on.

'Keep whatever you like,' he added.

A pretty red-haired girl came over. She peeled off the bra she was wearing and handed it to me, saying, 'I think this would look better on you.' Her name was Ashleigh.

I was still a little rocked emotionally from that morning's argument with Chris, but I pasted on a smile and, after a couple of glasses of champagne, my mood lifted and I began to enjoy myself.

Even though we were away from the elaborate security system of The Club, John and his two friends were incredibly kind and respectful of our unspoken 'No Touching' rule. Apart from the fact we were sprawled around a fancy hotel room, and the lighting wasn't quite as flattering, it was actually very similar to working in The Club. Ashleigh and I did a double show together – I busted out some naked handstands and left feeling like myself again – just $700 richer. Then I realised I'd have to explain to Chris where I had been all afternoon.

Chris may have taught me what the feeling of heart-fluttering love is. But it wasn't unconditional love. We were in love with each other's potential – the idea of who we could be 'if only …' Not with who we actually were.

In a strip club, everything is an equation – I will trade you fifteen minutes of my time, I will flirt with you and get naked for you. I will even share some of my 'self' with you, in return for some cold hard cash. Love is not an equation. Real life is not an equation. Just because I want something to work out in a particular way, does not mean it will.

I don't regret many things in my life, but if I could travel back in time and tell myself just one thing, it would be that Chris wasn't The One. In losing him, I felt that I had lost my chance at ever feeling love. Like I only got one shot at it, I had blown it and that was that. I wish I could tell my twenty-year-old self that there is not just 'One', that I would get the opportunity to be in love several more times over the course of my life. I didn't know this at the time, of course. I just had this feeling of a sinking black pit of despair, that I had destroyed this beautiful precious thing simply by being myself.

One of the hardest things we have to do in life is to turn around to the people who love us the most and say: 'This person that you want me to be? That is not who I am.' Partners and family members don't realise what is at stake when they ask you to give up parts of who you are, in order to meet their expectations of who they think you should be. Through losing Chris, the job I loved and my previously happy relationship with my parents, I almost lost everything.

Chris and I are having a fistfight at a friend's birthday party. I have so much rage and hatred towards him. I have given up everything for him. Everything that makes me, me. And it is still not enough. He still does not love me. My friend's dad pulls us apart to break up the fight. I have my keys. I get in my car and leave. It is a thirty-minute drive back to Mom's house and perhaps I can calm down on the way home. I don't. 'The Nanny Diaries' is playing through my car stereo and I barely hear it over the sound of my internal screaming – 'I'm going to die. I'm going to die.' I am determined.

I shower and wash my hair. I put on white pyjamas with strawberries on them and calmly gather all the pills I can find from around the house. Anti-depressants, sleeping pills, a whole packet of Panadol. I pop them methodically from their blister packets and choke down handfuls at a time, washing them down with huge swigs of peach schnapps. I scrawl a note saying *I am sorry.* I call Chris to say goodbye. He must have called my mom because she calls my phone a few minutes later to check I am OK. I reassure her that I am and she hangs up.

I pause.

I called her back. In a very small voice I tell her.

'I've taken pills. A lot of pills …'

I'm being manhandled by my stepdad into the car, then screeching through the streets late at night to the local hospital – already starting to drift in and out of consciousness. Bright lights. Slipping away again. I wake up momentarily. I am strapped down to a bed with tubes, so many tubes coming out of my mouth, arms, vagina. I struggle a little against the thick material but I am bound tightly. 'Like someone in a mental hospital,' I think then I pass out again.

I lose two whole days.

Chapter 7

Poles Apart.

I am 21 years old.

For my 21st birthday, my parents bought me a return ticket to Europe, on the condition that I never contact Chris again. They may have blamed him for my actions but, really, suicide is a simple equation: your pain exceeds your internal resources for coping with it. Their brave and beautiful gesture was the best thing they could have done for me.

I was keen to get away from the lingering memories of Chris and the black hole I had found myself in. Their generosity meant I could go somewhere where nobody knew Emma or Suzie, where I could re-create myself to be whoever I wanted. Nobody would know me, my story or my problems, because I only existed as a set of possibilities. It was like creating my backstory at The Club, only this time it was in real life. I was feeling a little reckless almost, like, 'F*** it, I should be dead anyway. This is bonus time.' So I bravely stepped out into the world, with only my backpack and a vague plan to visit Greece and London. I started my trip with friends on the Greek island of Mykonos. I began to deal with the stresses of travel almost immediately – my backpack had been misplaced on the journey and my friends greeted me at the ferry terminal, chanting: 'We are sexy, we are hot. We have luggage, you do not.'

I wrote weekly emails home to my family and friends, with tales of my adventures and noticed that the more 'stressful' the event, the better the story. It helped me step outside of my problems, like I was looking at them from another perspective. I began to look forward to things going 'wrong' and I wouldn't get upset or distressed, instead, I felt happy because I knew it would make a great story that I could share later.

Mykonos is perhaps not the greatest place for an introverted redhead. It is hot and bright. The white buildings shine like scoops of ice cream with vivid blue-colored toppings. My daytime option was to join the hordes of bikini-clad European women lounging in deck chairs along the beach, while overweight men with leathery skin surreptitiously studied the flesh on display from underneath their sun visors. Night-time saw the place become a party town – drinking and dancing in thumping, pumping clubs before sleeping away your hangover at the beach next day. Wash, rinse, repeat the next day, and the next … and next … ad nauseum.

True to form, I found a way to avoid both the Sun and the night-time shenanigans by working. Within a few days of my arrival I had secured myself a job dancing on a bar during the afternoons. It paid poorly (a few euros and free drinks) but gave me the sense of purpose that work always has always provided. *I am working. I am achieving. Therefore I am okay.* Plus, it was in the shade so my white skin retained its usual pallor. The locals found it amusing: 'You're Australian? But you're so pale!' and tried to entice me into the Sun – but I got burned even with sunscreen on and sitting under an umbrella. It was a relief to head to London, where my white skin was not such an anomaly.

My plan had always been to strip in the UK. I was keen to start feeling more like myself again and, as soon as I began work at a table-dancing club called The Pussycat Lounge in East London, I felt like I'd come home.

The Pussycat was great fun. The décor was pink and leopard print – from the carpet and the bar stools to the handrail of the stairs. We had to pay a house fee of £50 at the start of our shift, but everything we earned from the customers was in cash and was ours to keep. This was a great system for high earners – and it kind of pushed out the low earners. If you're naked and it's costing you money to go to work each night, you're not going to stay long. It was a relief to be earning pounds; my stash of cash I had brought over with me was dwindling.

Two storeys of railed balconies circled the towering poles, which ran up the center of the club with a cross bar connecting them. Girls would climb up one pole, disappearing from the sight of the ground-floor patrons as they became obscured by the first-floor balcony. They would shimmy across the cross bar and come sliding gracefully down the other pole. It was the same but different to home – there were no tips given onstage, instead, you took a 'collection' prior to your podiums, walking around with a pint glass into which customers dropped one- or two-pound coins. The gold coins made a particular 'thunk' sound as they dropped into the glass, so you knew when someone was trying to get away with dropping in some silver.

After my audition (I danced to 'Sk8ter Boy' by Avril Lavigne), we began the name discussion:

'I'm Suzie.'

'Sorry, we already have a Suzie.'

Oh God, here we go again.

This time Amber was available and finally, four years later than originally intended, I made my debut onstage as 'Amber'.

It turned out this was not such a good thing; I don't know if it was my accent, or the loud music, but this conversation happened several times each night:

'Hi there, my name is Amber.'

'Did you say Emma?'

'NO NO NO! I definitely did NOT say Emma …'

I had an innate abject revulsion to people using my real name. It freaked me out completely to hear the 'E-word' being used in a strip-club environment. She didn't belong in here. Emma was an identity I protected fiercely. No one had access to her unless they earned it.

Having spent the past few years being Suzie, trying to change names again was confusing, especially after a champagne or three. I would get mixed up and introduce myself as 'Suzamber.' After a couple of shifts, I just sort of gave up and let slip my 'real' name (Suzie) to any customer I was selling to. Private shows were only one song (three minutes), which we timed ourselves, so it was very much up to me to get the customer to extend. After being used to doing fifteen-minute shows, I almost felt I was ripping the customers off dancing for such a short period of time. I used this to my advantage: 'I've barely taken my knickers off – you have to stay for another show!' The main downside of The Pussycat was that, for licensing reasons, floor-work was prohibited, which literally meant you couldn't go on your knees, or lie down on your back, when you were dancing. My feet hated it. Floor-work is the only break you get from your six-inch heels and, at the end of each seven-hour shift, I was blistered, bleeding and in an inordinate amount of pain. In the interests of saving my poor feet, I always zeroed in on customers who were seated on the leopard-print lounges, especially those who had a spare chair beside them.

'Hi there, mind if I sit down? My feet are killing me.'

'I think I see the problem,' the customer replied in a posh English accent, gesturing to my feet. 'You're wearing stilts instead of shoes.'

'Regulation uniform, I'm afraid. These are my work boots. I'm Amber by the way, but my real name's Suzie. What do you do?'

'I work for a bank.'

'Ah, finance … investments?'

'Tea and coffee.'

'That's very admirable, starting at the bottom and working your way up.'

'Absolutely, I'm hoping to branch out into biscuits soon.'

'Answer me, honestly, does that line ever work for you?'

'Actually, I usually tell people I'm an astronaut.'

'Seriously?'

'Yes, you just have to be believable about it. I tell them I work for NASA and that I'm 46th in line to go into space so it's unlikely I'll ever get out there – but I'm still technically an astronaut.'

With his ability to bullshit, flirt and make me smile, this guy would have made a great table dancer.

...

I finished up my time in London and exchanged my British pounds for dollars. With the exchange rate, taking my clothes off in Mother England had proved quite lucrative; my apartment was getting closer. Back home, my black cloud lifted. My parents had been right in buying me that plane ticket. It had given me a global perspective on my very local problems. I vowed that, if ever I considered taking my life again, I would take off instead and start life over under a new name, with a new identity – away from my old world and perceived problems. Existing as a set of infinite possibilities is liberating. I felt re-energised and excited to re-engage with my life and friends. I completed two Certifications in Fitness so I could become an Aerobics Instructor and Personal Trainer, and threw myself back into work at The Club and the pub circuit.

I resumed the Friday pole classes with Bobbi and, sometimes, the odd non-industry woman would join us. Coming into the secret world of The Club when it was closed and doing a 'pole-dancing hens' night' was becoming increasingly popular – complete with complimentary champagne and a Feature Show from Bobbi herself. So popular, in fact, that one of the women who had come along convinced Bobbi to go into business with her, setting up Australia's first designated pole-dancing school. I was desperate to be involved. I loved teaching fitness classes – getting a bunch of people up and moving gave me the same buzz that I got from being onstage, and I loved the feeling of flying around the poles. Here was a way to combine the two things and also to experience employment that allowed me to keep my pants on.

I collected Bobbi's costume as usual after her next show. I was determined to ask her for a job, but got too nervous. I ended up asking about which class I could take at her school instead. It was Ashleigh (who was already teaching for Bobbi) who spoke on my behalf and secured my new position as a 'Pole Instructor'.

When I rocked up to teach my first class, I really didn't know what I was doing. We did a full aerobics-style warm up complete with grapevines and star jumps, then I taught them the moves and routine Bobbi had shown me. Her studio was like the ultimate princess bedroom I'd always wanted as a little girl – painted a soft pastel pink with flattering lighting provided by pink-colored lamps in each corner. The windows had pink chiffon and sequinned curtains and there was a change room with a mirrored vanity. Evenly spaced around the room was a mix of spinning and static 38 mm brass poles. Girls booked in for an eight-week course; they'd come in wearing their business suits or 'mom clothes' and emerge from the change room in hot pants and towering high heels. This was Secret Women's Business – the almost-clandestine nature of the studio (located on the top floor of an older-style office building) made it feel like a secret society, a club to which only women could belong, a safe place to express their sexuality and release their inhibitions. I felt like I was part of something important.

After a few months of teaching, I learned that getting a forty- or fifty-year-old woman out of track pants and into booty shorts – in front of other people – *is* important. These women had not felt confident enough to parade around in a bra and hot pants for a long time. If ever.

I was teaching women to writhe like strippers inside the protected pink bubble of the pole studio. They stared at me with focused determination, trying to emulate my undulations and body rolls like I had mimicked Jasmine at my audition – but I didn't completely understand. I did this sexy dance for money. Why were they doing it?

Slowly, it began to dawn on me. They weren't strippers. They had never stood up naked in front of people and had hundreds of strangers tell them over and over they were beautiful. The pole studio is another contrived, controlled environment, where it is okay to be sexual. It is okay to be sexy. Without having that sexual behavior put them at risk. It was a chance for them to be told, 'Hey – you're okay! Even those parts you keep hidden – those parts are okay, too!' Pole dancing helped them appreciate the amazing things their bodies could do, rather than what they looked like.

Apart from the occasional male student, the studio was predominantly for women only. When we danced, it wasn't for men, it wasn't for money, it was for ourselves.

Watching my students strut their stuff on their 'Graduation' performance night at the end of each eight-week term, I felt like a proud mom. Teaching aerobics, I was improving women's body shapes. Teaching pole dancing, I was not only doing that, I was also improving their body confidence and self-esteem. I had the most rewarding job in the world. I began to teach higher levels, beyond Beginners. I still didn't really know what I was doing – but had long since mastered the art of 'faking it until you make it'. My fitness certifications had given me a basic understanding of human anatomy and movement so I would explain the dynamics of difficult moves, lying on my back on the floor to avoid demonstrating moves I had not yet mastered myself. I stayed back after classes ended to practice and practice. I even thumbtacked a piece of string into the ceiling at home and marked out choreography for class routines around my 'pole'.

My weeks were a mix of teaching pole classes and pole-dancing hens' nights, doing pub shows and two to three shifts at The Club each week, as well as still forging ahead with my degree. I sometimes wondered if I was teaching the Hen to pole dance in the afternoon before stripping for the Buck at The Club later that night.

The bulk of what I earned was tipped into my ever-growing savings account – I had been to see several banks and mortgage brokers, only to be rejected each time because I was technically self-employed (on the form I said I was a promotional model). The majority of my income came through the business of being Suzie Q. And the banks didn't like it. It got to the point where I had more than half the purchase price for a property saved up before finally, finally, one Bank Manager said 'yes' (probably because he was a friend of a friend and the two of us went into the bank and quite literally begged).

With my finance secured, I went shopping. The best kind of shopping … apartment shopping.

During the week, I scoured the real-estate section of the newspaper and property websites. I researched median house prices, capital growth areas and proposed public transport services and arterial roads. I even got my Certificate in Real Estate Practice so I would know about relevant legislation and the business of real estate.

I carefully scheduled my weekends to fit in as many 'Open for Inspections' in my preferred areas as possible. Everyone had an opinion about what I should buy and where. But I told them all: I would 'know it when I see it.'

And I did.

It was a small older-style one-bedroom unit, close to a public transport, surrounded by beautiful local parks and only half an hour from the center of the city. It had new carpet and fresh paint. I walked inside and instantly felt like I was home. It was perfect.

The day I got the keys, I was adamant that I would sleep there. I had no fridge or furniture, just a foam mattress on the floor in the corner of the bedroom. I lay there, staring up at the vermiculite ceiling, thinking, *Finally a home that's all mine. No one can ask me to leave.* I felt happy and safe.

I was too excited to sleep. I had finally done it! I was a home owner! I had worked so hard to get a mortgage and now I just wanted to pay it off and rid myself of it quickly as possible.

As soon as I had all my furniture moved in and set up, I had a pole installed.

I could now practice my class routines properly (well, sort of … when I went upside down, one foot went in my wardrobe and the other almost went out the window). I loved pole dancing. It was acrobatic, sexy and becoming a great way to earn a living. It was catching on as a form of exercise and as an art form, beyond the strip clubs that had birthed it. In 2005 I competed in the first-ever Miss Pole Dance Australia competition. It was held at the Bourbon and Beefsteak in Kings Cross (a far cry from the glamorous Enmore Theatre where it is held today). I did a Pink Panther–inspired routine and placed second to Jamilla Deville. I won the title of 'Best Entertainer' – I was thrilled. Here were some of the best pole dancers and I was up there onstage with them and, not only that, the judges thought mine was the most entertaining show! Just as Lynda told me, people are there to be entertained. In every show I have ever done, on a pole or taking my clothes off, entertaining the crowd is my number-one priority. I play characters and tell stories. Performing onstage is when I am completely in the flow. Filled with joy, happiness and complete and total presence. Just like when I was onstage at The Club, I make eye contact with as many people as possible. Inviting them into my world for a few moments so they can share my elation with me.

A couple of weeks after the competition, Bobbi got in touch with me about a television opportunity. The contract was for two separate reality TV series that would be filmed back-to-back here and overseas.

The first series was called *Travel Girls*. It was a competition between five girls who wanted to be travel presenters – like on *Getaway*. Bubbly girls who loved travel and were happy to talk on camera? *Yes! That's me!* I thought.

The second series was called *Tour Girls III* and was commissioned by Playboy TV. The premise was simple: load a bunch of strippers and porn stars into a mini-van and take them on a stripping tour around pubs, filming their boobs and backstage dramas. The first show definitely sounded more appealing than the second.

The catch was, you had to do both.

I wondered how many other strippers out there were interested in being TV presenters – or even how many would actually be happy and comfortable being filmed? I'd now accepted that I was a 'lifer' in the industry – having images of my naked body captured forever on film no longer fazed me. I wasn't worried about it coming back to bite me in a future career, because this *was* my career. I figured that, when I was too old to strip anymore, I would become the Madame of a high-end brothel.

Still on my high of 'I'm on bonus time anyway', and totally determined to embrace every opportunity that came my way, I signed the contract, agreeing to both shows.

As it turned out, my skillset was indeed unique. Not a single one of the other girls had ever stripped before. None of us had any idea where we would be going or what we would be doing, just that we would all be meeting in Thailand on a particular date. This was part of the show: challenges and locations would be revealed on air so as to capture our reactions. I was told to pack clothing for 'temperatures ranging from zero degrees to thirty degrees.'

I was given a crash course in the constructed reality of a TV reality series. 'I'm sorry, can you two please have that conversation again? The microphone wasn't recording.' 'Okay, do that again so we can film it from a different angle.' *Travel Girls* was a reality TV series about making a reality TV series – everyone made daily video diaries – not just the girls but also the producers and camera crew.

Because all the girls were doing both TV series, we did our promotional shoot for *Tour Girls III* on a deserted beach in Phuket. It was my first time posing nude for a camera and I loved it. The make-up and hair artists made me feel like a movie star. The photographer had flown in from Los Angeles especially to shoot us. He was friendly and made me giggle every time he wanted to do a nude shot, because he called out, 'Okay, show me your cookie.' I felt completely comfortable in front of the camera. It felt similar to posing for a life modelling class, only a little more exotic – we drank out of coconuts and posed in the crystal-clear water and on the warm sand.

Travel Girls was one of those epic, once-in-a-lifetime opportunities. I got to ride an elephant in Thailand; I was backstage at the Lido in Paris to interview one of the dancers; I was flown in a helicopter over the Great Barrier Reef. I got into trouble from a Producer for walking 'too much like a stripper' down Whitehaven beach in the Whitsundays (I didn't really know how to walk any other way). And I was even felt up by a sea lion at Seaworld! The only dark moment happened on the final leg of our journey.

We stopped off in Bangkok once more and went to see the girls performing in the Red Light District of Patpong. These were the notorious 'ping pong' shows and involved the girls expelling everything from darts to coca cola out of their genitalia. The expressions on their faces were a mix of boredom and misery. It was the first time I had seen women not gleefully choosing to work in the sex industry. I realised that, although back home my stripper friends and I had choices and other options for our lives and careers, these women did not. It was a sobering thought. I tipped them with all my remaining money and left, disturbed by what I had seen, but not really sure what I could do to fix it.

We filmed the finale episode in Australia. I placed second and I cried. I had tried so hard – forgoing nights out with the crew to be fresh-faced for the camera in the morning, keeping up my intense fitness regime in our tiny Parisian hotel. I really had had my heart set on winning and here I was, Second Place again.

I was pulled aside by a producer and given a partial explanation – I had not been forthcoming enough with my back-story. I had not opened up enough about who I was on-camera. For me, being on-camera was like performing – I flicked the 'Suzie Switch' and was instantly bright, bubbly and cheerful. Anything beyond that was Emma. And I was sure people didn't want to see Emma. After all, Emma had her period. Emma had bad days. Emma fought with her boyfriend. Emma was not always having fun. Emma felt personal, private – but that was what viewers were after – a glimpse into who you really were.

Lesson learned.

I braced myself for *Tour Girls*. I had the feeling it wouldn't be the joyful exotic romp that *Travel Girls* had been.

I was right.

One of the girls had a complete breakdown, saying she could not possibly get naked on camera. She left in tears, flying back home.

This left us short one stripper. The solution? Fly in one short stripper..

A 5-foot tall, gorgeous, exotic dancer, named Phoenix Knight, to the rescue.

This was actually her real name – because who needs a stripper name when your real name is that awesome? Phoenix was like a beautiful ray of sunshine pouring into my life. After four weeks of being essentially on the outer, choosing not to socialise with the girls and crew had had a cost. I felt like I had met my spirit animal. Phoenix was

– and still is – the ultimate pocket rocket and we became inseparable almost immediately – finally, another actual stripper! Someone who I had a shared commonality with – the instant sisterhood that forms when you recognise in another an identical willingness to sell a glimpse of her private parts.

We flew out to New Zealand and were loaded into the tour bus (hired campervan) and then drove for five hours to our first venue and our first performance. The producers waited until we were fully made up and warmed up, ready to go, before letting us know the venue had cancelled our show. We glared at them from under our fake eyelashes.

This pretty much set the tone for two hateful weeks of filming, where the producers tried to provoke us into dramatic reactions on camera – all in the name of 'good TV'. They didn't use our names – we were referred to as 'whore' or 'slut'. I threw my recent resolution – to 'expose who I really was on camera' – out the window. I put my head down, resolved to do my strip shows to the best of my ability, and tried not to tread on anyone's toes. I vowed to get away from these awful people as soon as possible.

I was there to earn as much money as I could by taking my clothes off and lap dancing men. I was obstinate in my video diaries, declining to answer their stupid questions – 'How many sex toys do you own? What are your biggest turn-ons? Share a sexual fantasy with us.' They were filming me naked, being a badass stripper. That was it. They weren't getting access to my personal sex life. They weren't getting access to me.

The one blessing to come out of the whole sordid ordeal was Phoenix. Crisis situations and dire circumstances force intimacy; we were best friends before we knew it. We shared a bed most nights.

In the wee hours of the morning, the cameraman would sneak in to film us, hopefully hooking up with each other or at least be in a compromising position. We never were, but perception is everything in the world of reality TV – editing can manipulate any situation to appear in whatever way best suits the show's storyline.

We drove for up to ten hours a day. I usually buried my head in a book at the back of the van, occasionally looking up to make some snarky comment. One night, they parked the van under a bridge for us to sleep 'like so many hobos before us'. We ate whatever we could forage at service stations; we stopped at caravan parks to shower before performing at one of a chain of pubs, all aptly named 'The Grumpy Mole'. We caught a few hours of sleep in the van before hitting the road again, only to repeat the whole process the next day at a new location.

I didn't embrace the experience at all. It was the first time I had felt truly exploited as a stripper. I was yelled at and treated with zero respect. Despite their best efforts to provoke us, it seemed we weren't providing enough 'drama', as in fighting or arguments. And so, a famous American porn star was flown in. She arrived, got drunk, lap danced one of the producers, fought with the other one, then passed out and fell off the side of the bed. I have a very clear memory of the head producer walking past me in the hotel's corridor, rubbing his hands together gleefully like some kind of cartoon villain, muttering, 'Great TV. This is *great* TV.'

Phoenix and I kept to ourselves. When the other girls went out drinking, we visited a local park. I taught her some pole tricks on the children's play equipment; she taught me some floor-work on towels spread out over the grass. Giggling and pulling sexy poses with our legs apart in the sunshine was the most fun I had on the trip.

She explained to me that, in addition to stripping, she'd also done photo shoots in *The Picture* and *People* magazines: 'It's great babe, really easy – you do a few shoots during the day and get paid depending on how many pics they use. If they use you on the cover, it can be up to a few grand.'

I saw dollar signs.

I had loved the break overseas; I was starting to tire of working in The Club. Being small, bouncy and FUN – night after night after night – was getting exhausting. I was running out of enthusiasm for meeting and greeting new people. It got to the point where I'd get ready, stick my head out of the change room and, if I didn't see any of my Regulars or anyone I knew, I'd duck back in and down a glass of wine, thoughtfully purchased for me by one of the Bar Flies (there was still no way I was paying for my own drinks at work).

Not only did I want to grow my property portfolio, I also wanted to experience all aspects of this industry, which was slowly becoming part of the fabric of my being. In order to earn money while still 'performing', I began to do Strippergrams. Strippergrams, or 'Grams' as they are known in the industry, are strip shows performed at a private residence or hotel room. R-rated shows are full nude, whereas X-rated shows involve some kind of insertion. Basically, you drive yourself to someone's house/boat/workplace and take your clothes off for fifteen minutes. They were an exercise in adaptability more than anything. You never quite knew what you were walking into when you knocked on the door. It could be an eighteenth birthday party, where the teenage girls clung a little tighter to their boyfriends (just in case), where the birthday boy's mom or grandma would pick up your G-string and costume pieces for you, delivering them to the bedroom where you stood butt-naked, covered in sweat and panting. Unzipping your thigh-high boots to reveal two pairs of football socks and kneepads. You danced in people's backyards – negotiating your way around white plastic chairs to lap dance excited men, ignoring the death stares from less-than-excited women, and keeping all your weight in your toes so your six-inch heels didn't sink into the grass. Warehouses where there was no stereo or sound system – my little boom box was so pitiful that one of the guys offered to 'back the ute up and turn the speakers up real loud.'

I might be performing what looks like a sexy act – but it's an imitation of sex that isn't really sex at all. I repeated the same 'sexual' manoeuvres ten to twenty times per night. I was not turned on. I was performing a carefully choreographed routine. Balancing naked upside down in someone's lap, or spinning around on my hands on a table before landing in a perfectly executed splits, is hard and takes practiced skills. I am *not* thinking about sex. I am thinking about how much longer I have left of the song, and where my moisturiser is so I can pour it over my breasts at the song's climactic point. The key is to not take off a single item of clothing for the whole first song. Tease them, lift up your skirt, flash your nipples, but don't actually strip anything off. Think about it; when you undress at home for a shower it takes you what – ten seconds, twenty seconds? Try taking a full fifteen minutes – and making sure it's entertaining the whole time. I'm serious. Time yourself. Fifteen minutes is a long time when all you are essentially doing is getting naked. Hence the 'tricks'.

You are naked but it's not sexy. Unlike in The Club, people who book a Strippergram are not wanting to be turned on; they want to see the Buck/Birthday Boy humiliated. And so you oblige. You ride the poor guy like a pony, whip him, soak him with bathwater, burn his chest hair off (you light hair mousse then keep it moving quickly so the skin doesn't burn), or rip his underwear off. There is no golden glow or magic bubble like what you create in a Private Show.

I once did a double show with my by-now best friend Ashleigh. She went to perform the underwear ripping move – you put the Buck on all-fours, shuffle the waistband of his underwear above the waistband of his pants, then 'heave-ho-pull'. Chances are, they're old and daggy and tear in half so you can pull the whole lot off over his head. Only this night, we were entertaining a lovely group of mathematicians (really) and the Buck must have been wearing a brand-new set of underwear. When Ashleigh went to rip, his back half lifted clear off the floor and I swear his eyes bulged almost out of his head. She'd delivered what must have been the most atomic wedgie ever given to another human being. I hope his new wife wasn't expecting too much action on their wedding night!

At another booking, a lovely group of young guys had heard I was a pole dancer and made me a pole – they'd stolen a stop sign and somehow secured it into a little wooden stage – they'd even installed lights onto the stage.

These bookings were organised through striptease agencies; the same ones that organised the pub shows each week. Guys (and it was always, invariably, guys) could book topless, lingerie and even nude waitresses, sexy poker dealers, and R- and X-rated strippers.

I was waitressing at a Buck's party once and the guys had also booked an X-rated girl – Paris – to perform an 'insertion' show. After dancing around the room dressed as a cop, she removed her clothes and lay on her back with legs akimbo as she coyly slid a lollipop all the way into her vagina, pulled it out and threw it into the hands of the Buck. He stared at it wide-eyed for a moment, amid the raucous whistling, cheering and cries of 'Eat it!' from his mates. He paused for a couple of seconds, before finally caving under the peer pressure and popped it into his mouth. Paris instantly stopped her sexy writhing on the floor. She stood up. Breaking the stripper illusion completely, she put her hands on her hips and shook her head at him. Her upper lip pulled back over her perfect white teeth in a snarl of absolute revulsion.

'That's Dis-Gus-Ting,' she said, carefully annunciating each syllable. 'You have *no* idea where I've been.'

The guys all laughed, but I couldn't help but feel like she had a point.

Unsure if she was joking or not, the guy offered the lollipop back to her.

She recoiled in horror.

'I have no idea where *you've* been either.'

She then calmly continued on with her show.

Saturday nights were filled with as many Grams as you could handle; I usually only took on about five. But as you drove all over, your phone beeped as more requests came in. You said 'yes' to the extra work because it was there and, gradually, your schedule would get pushed out later and later – the jobs always took longer than expected because no one could work the stereo, someone stole your G-string or they couldn't find the guy with the cash (always get cash up front). This is why strippers are notoriously late. Stripper time says, 'Yes, I'll be there by 11 p.m.,' even though I am ninety minutes away and it is currently 10:45 p.m. You called the customer when you were about half an hour away, reassuring him you were 'just around the corner'.

In terms of income, Saturday night equated to an entire working week and, as it only came around once every seven days, you wanted to say 'yes' as much as you could. Your body grew hot then cold, hot then cold, as your adrenaline spiked up then down, up then down, all night. It took me a few hours to unwind after I had finished work and I would be exhausted on Sunday and into Monday as well.

Drugs were commonplace – I was occasionally offered them at The Club and at almost every Strippergram I ever did. I think it's an all-or-nothing approach – you either say yes every time, or no every time. At five to ten jobs a night, that's potentially a lot of cocaine. And it's free.

I opted for 'no every time'.

For a couple of months, I still had Sunday morning pole classes at Bobbi's. I was never one to refuse work, but it was hard. All my jobs required me to be 'on', even when I'd only finished stripping a couple of hours before. I stood in front of an eager group of students, wearing my black sunglasses, one hand wrapped firmly around a double-shot latte, wondering why on Earth anyone wanted to pole dance at 8 a.m. on a Sunday morning. At least I wasn't hung over. No more sipping champagne for me. I now spent the majority of my Saturday nights in the car, racing around the city from job to job. I lasted one torturous term of this before asking Bobbi, 'Please don't roster me on for mornings again. Ever.'

Being so busy and being around men at their worst (drunk, horny and raucous) began to spill over into my personal life. Mentally, I began to divide men into Type A and Type B. Type B were those who 'got it' – they understood it was an act. That it wasn't who I was. Type A, on the other hand, equated what they saw onstage with who I was as a person.

Disappointingly, Type A seemed to be about 99 per cent of the male population.

Eager to understand why my job caused so much discord in my personal and familial relationships, I wrote an essay on the social and economic capital of sex workers as one of my final assignments at uni. The key idea behind it was that, in most sectors of society, if you amass economic capital (money) and cultural capital (education, knowledge and skills), then there is a corresponding increase in your social capital (social status). Except, if you work in the sex industry. I think my lecturer was really impressed that I had interviewed all these real-life sex workers (my friends). There was one especially in-depth interview – with the exotic dancer 'Suzie Q' – who really opened up about what it was like to work in the industry.

I received top marks. But no greater understanding of why my job caused so much discord in those around me. Things only mean what you make them mean. Although to me stripping meant one thing (money, fun, performing), to my parents, family and society at large it meant something else entirely.

My pole career was starting to take off at this point – people enjoyed my show at Miss Pole Dance Australia and I was flown interstate, and even overseas, to teach pole workshops and perform. I performed pole at a corporate event at the Hilton Hotel in Mombai, India. We were put up in a five-star hotel, with full access to an incredible buffet for each meal, and I began to taste the life that Richard had introduced me to. Only this time I was providing it for myself. I had really enjoyed my time overseas filming *Travel Girls* and I wanted to see more of the world. Paying for travel would have taken precious financial resources away from my property portfolio fund. I wondered, *Could I be paid to travel?*

Could I be a jet-setting stripper and pole dancer?

The next week, after my beautiful time in India performing onstage with singers and back-up dancers, I was sinking my heels into the mud in someone's backyard as I danced for a Buck who had to be woken up from his drunken stupor so I could lap dance him.

The contrast was jarring.

It was time to stop doing Grams.

Glen Woodhead

Age 8, upside down in my underwear, 1990. Pretty much the theme for my life.

Miss Nude Australia 2007!

Age 11, graduating Year 6 in 1994, and I'm already on a pole!

Sputnik

Taking the stage at the finals of Miss Nude Australia, 2007.

Richard Arthur/Penthouse Australia

My *Penthouse* cover, 2008. Makeup and airbrushing means the girl in the magazine doesn't even look like the girl in the magazine!

Tony Hunter/ The Picture Magazine

Photoshoot in a luxury waterfront mansion, 2008. Wondering if I would be able to afford this house one day!

I always felt like I was flying when I was performing on a pole, 2009.

Mucking around on stage in a strip club with Skunkers - a toy skunk who used to accompany me on my travels, 2009

Promo shoots with Toby J, 2011. The pole may just have been the third member of our relationship.

"Are you guys Avatar?" Backstage at the Asia Pacific Pole Championships, 2010.

Justin Tran

Thighs of steel! Promo shoot with Toby J, 2012.

Vertigo Photography

Being naked on stage naked was no worries – but those first few times as an MC were petrifying, 2012.

Toby J

The glamorous life of a pole studio owner. Painting the bathrooms at Suzie Q Pole Studio, 2013.

Eros Shine Awards

On the red carpet with Toby J at the Eros Shine Awards. I won 'Best Performance Artist' and took a toy dog as my handbag, 2012.

Toby J

Grinning my head off after performing for Bono, 2012.

Millie Robson

Teaching a class at Suzie Q Pole Studio, 2013.

Vertigo Photography

Creating a name for myself in the niche market of 'Pole MC', 2014.

Pole Candy, 2014. Dad: "Is that all you're wearing?"

Nervous before you go onstage? Just picture everyone in their underwear, 2014..

Recreating myself as Emma – still with a touch of Suzie Q, 2015.

Jenelle Stafford

Social media shoot for my studio to try and increase student numbers, 2015.

Roberto Duran

Shooting as Emma ...with wings! Naked in my parents' backyard (they weren't home), 2016.

Sexpo South Africa

At Sexpo in Johannesburg. One of my last times on stage as a showgirl, 2016.

Still upside down in my underwear. Performing with Mark and Lani DeViate at Hellfire, 2016.

The 'Emma' shoot that *Penthouse* were interested in. I look calm, but that pond weed was pretty gross, 2016.

Chapter 8

That's Not My Vagina!

I am 23 to 25 years old.

I was offered another reality TV series.

My initial response was an emphatic, 'No! No! No!' After the hellish nightmare of *Tour Girls*, I didn't want anything to do with people stressing out strippers in the name of entertainment. I called the producer and was instantly flooded with relief when a woman answered the phone. She reassured me that this show was about celebrating exotic dance and would be nothing like my previous experience. The concept was like *Australian Idol* for strippers – eight strippers living in a waterfront mansion in for two weeks. Each day, we would be put through a series of stripping 'challenges'. Ashleigh would be joining me – in fact, almost all the girls in the house had been on the circuit with me. The prize for the winner? $25K cash and a brand new car.

The title of the show: *Erotic Star*.

I plunged back into the realm of 'reality' TV. Our first challenge was to run a Bikini Car Wash. Havoc ensued – unleashing a bunch of wet, soapy, highly competitive strippers on the unsuspecting general public is a recipe for both drama and entertainment. We caused a minor car accident as one male driver took his eyes off the road for a little too long, watching our shenanigans with the water hose.

We went speed dating, belly dancing and performed our strip shows on a boat cruising Sydney Harbour. I survived elimination after elimination, and made it to the Grand Final. I burst into tears when they announced I was going through. It really does feel like your entire life and career is on the line when you're in the pressure-cooker environment of a reality TV series.

The Grand Final was filmed some weeks later. It came down to four of us – myself, Ashleigh, Sasha and Trinity Porter. I went to see my mentor, Gayna Galaxy. She loaned me a spectacular costume from Thailand. Huge wings that were so sparkly my eyes hurt and a headpiece she'd made. I showed her my choreography; she helped me polish it up and gave me a 'secret recipe' (six bags of glitter into half a bottle of baby oil) for the climax of my show. The whole act was carefully orchestrated – I wouldn't be able to touch the pole once I was covered in glittery baby oil, so my pole tricks had to come early on in the performance – not too early though, because I wanted enough time to show off my massive, beautiful costume. You need to pole dance in as little as possible because your skin is what helps you grip to the pole – our entire show was only six minutes.

I had some special wooden cups made to hold dry ice in. From behind the bar at The Oxford Tavern, I collected some empty Jim Beam bottles and tied white ribbons around them. They were filled with hot water (I even brought a kettle with me backstage), which I tipped it into the wooden bowls to create a spectacular and dramatic smoky effect around me. Sasha spent close to $10K on her show, with back-up dancers and a massive champagne glass that she sat in and poured bubbly champagne over herself. I spent 50 bucks on my dry ice.

I won.

For the first time in my life, I hadn't come second. My bridesmaid spell was over.

I still had that sneaky 'Ha ha! I can't believe they bought it! Look at what I'm getting away with' feeling and was grinning like an idiot as I accepted my giant novelty cheque for $25,000.

The whole lot went straight onto my mortgage.

Still on a high from the confidence boost of winning *Erotic Star*, I decided to have another crack at the Miss Nude Australia title. This time at least, I hoped, I would make it to the National Final. I took my preparations seriously – very seriously. I spoke to every girl I could find who had ever entered the competition, questioning them about their experiences and what they thought made a winner. The advice ranged from: 'Get acrylic nails so your hands look nice as you run them over your boobs,' to 'Sex face. It's all about the sex face. Perfect that and the title is yours.'

I memorised the judging criteria, then built my show around it – ten points each for Body, Facial Beauty, Talent, Personality and Beauty Queen Image. I began to take lessons in aerial hoop (Lyra) to add some extra skills and hopefully increase my points in the 'Talent' category. I cut back my upper-body training because I felt too much muscle wasn't in line with a 'Beauty Queen Image'. Even though I had my own fitness qualifications, I hired a personal trainer to make sure I scored as high as possible in the 'Body' category.

I even took a private lesson with Ashleigh to perfect my all-important 'sex face'. After sixty minutes that essentially consisted of making orgasm faces at each other and giggling, I had it down. I sourced a sponsor to pay for my hotel room. The Crazy Horse (the club that hosted the competition) provided shared accommodation for all the competitors, but I wanted my own space so I could stay well rested and completely focused.

I adapted and extended the show I had used for *Erotic Star* (it had to be twelve minutes this time). I lived and breathed my show. I listened to the music when I was cleaning my apartment; I used the track as a warm-up for my pole classes; I practiced in my lounge room, at the pole studio and in the car.

I won Miss Nude NSW and was awarded 'Hottest Body' – thank you, Mr Trainer. I barely took the time to acknowledge or celebrate my victory. I was completely focused on the National Final. Winning the State heat was simply a necessary step on the path to success. As luck would have it, a film crew decided to make a documentary about the competition, so my journey towards the title is captured forever in a documentary entitled *Best Undressed*. It still screens on SBS from time to time. I was honest on camera, letting them see a bit of Emma, my real self and opinions, rather than just answering, 'I like sex and being tied up.' I was very keen for people to see what it was really like behind the scenes – to show the general public that strippers are people, too.

Miss Nude Australia is a gruelling week of competition. On the Sunday, fourteen finalists from all over Australia are flown into The Crazy Horse (Australia's oldest strip club) in Adelaide. On Monday night we all show up, made up, primped, primed and ready to go – and only seven names are drawn out of a hat to actually compete with their shows. It's incredibly nerve-wracking, not even knowing if you're going to perform that night, but having to be completely prepared and ready, just in case. On Tuesday, the remaining seven girls compete. On Wednesday, you all show up once again, ready to go, and only seven names are drawn; the other seven from this second draw compete on the Thursday night. The top two placing performers from each night make it through to the final on the Friday night. So you can qualify, fly all the way to Adelaide and not even compete in the actual 'Final' of Miss Nude Australia. I was determined that this would not be me and set my sights on not just gracing, but completely rocking, the stage on Friday night.

Each night, whether or not you're doing your show, you're required to do 'parades'. Just like in the Miss Universe pageant, there is an evening-wear parade and a swimwear parade. Unlike the Miss Universe pageant, there is also a full nude parade. As the name implies, you all walk around the stage before lining up with numbers on your wrists, a little bit like meat at auction, to have your breasts, butts, legs and bodies judged for the minor titles: 'Best Breasts' (more commonly referred to as 'Luscious Lungs'), 'Best Butt' and 'Best Entertainer'. I figured that, if I didn't win the big title, then 'Best Entertainer' would be the next best thing.

I was friendly with the other contestants, but didn't really socialise with them outside of the competition. I essentially spent the entire week trying to preserve my spray tan. Since Rebecca's advice at my first audition, I knew the ins and outs of tanning moisturisers, mousses, sprays and lotions. I hadn't been able to sleep on white bed sheets or own white clothing since I began stripping. The week of Miss Nude I barely showered and, on the nights I wasn't competing, I slathered myself in an obscene amount of moisturiser so I didn't look patchy for the final.

Friday rolled around. I woke early. I made myself a cup of tea and waited impatiently for the clock to hit 8 a.m., the earliest I could call to see if I had made it through. The phone rang and my heart thumped loudly. A dry voice unenthusiastically told me that I had made it. I was competing in the finals of Miss Nude Australia! Beaming down the phone, I thanked him, hung up, whooped and cheered, high five-ing myself as I jumped around the apartment.

At the club that night, there was a mix of joy and disappointment among the finalists and those missing out. We pulled numbers out of a hat to determine our order. I pulled out seven. My birthdate! *Surely this is a sign?* Not only that, I was second last! Second last is a great position in a competition. The crowd is relaxed and more vocal, and the judges tend to judge the first few performers harshly before they establish their median scores.

I sailed confidently through my parades, arching my back like a cat to make my butt look as perky as possible in the cattle auction. I took my time preparing my body with a slow warm-up backstage for the main event. The crowd was *on point* – I could hear roars and screams of approval echoing backstage. I kept focus on my body and my breathing. Trying to keep my nerves under control.

One of the girls had a disaster. Her CD started looping, playing the same section of her song over and over. Like some stripper hell, she was trapped in eternal purgatory of the same eight bars of 'I Love the Nightlife.' When she came offstage, she was in tears. All that hard work – wasted. A few of the girls brought their boyfriends, friends and even parents along. I was alone.

One of the girl's partners commented, 'She'll get a rock when she's finished with all this,' as he gestured vaguely around the club.

Suddenly, I was glad that I was alone. That would never be good enough for me. I expected unconditional love.

Even if I am a stripper.

My music started. I took a deep breath and entered the stage. Everything went smoothly. I flew up and down the poles, and removed my G-string dramatically while upside down in my Lyra. I remembered my 'sex face'. Most importantly – I had fun! There sometimes comes a moment onstage, the moment when you realise you can do no wrong – the audience is with you, on your side, willing you to succeed. I call it the 'Yes Factor'.

My show had the Yes Factor.

Backstage, my heart was thumping nervously in my chest when they started to announce the minor titles. I was awarded 'Best Butt'. I grinned and mentally thanked my trainer as I accepted my trophy. I crossed my fingers, silently hoping for 'Entertainer of the Year', which would essentially mean I performed the judges' favorite show. I tried to feel happy for one of the girls from Darwin when she was awarded this title but, secretly, I was disappointed.

Then I feel a little flame start to flicker in the pit of my stomach. They announce third place. The flame starts to grow stronger. They announce second place. I am praying to the Stripper Gods. My whole body feels alive with adrenaline. It's lit up with a burning sensation from inside … Maybe … Maybe … 'Miss Nude Australia is … Suzie Q!'

I had done it! This was the absolute pinnacle of my whole career! The blood roared in my ears as I was pushed out onto the stage. Some girls cry when they win. But I couldn't wipe the big goofy smile off my face. I mouthed, *Thank you*, at the judges while last year's winner placed a huge crown on my head.

'Good luck,' she whispered in my ear as I collected another novelty cheque and stood in stunned amazement.

Offstage, I began texting my friends, and then called my dad.

'Dad, Dad – I won Miss Nude Australia! I AM Miss

Nude Australia!'

'Hmmm ... Okay, Em–'

'Dad, I won twenty thousand dollars!'

'OH, MY GOD WHAT?! That is fantastic. You've almost got enough for your second apartment deposit now. I am so proud of you!'

I celebrated quietly with some chamomile tea and a soothing bubble bath. I know I've just unlocked the door to a whole new world of opportunity and travel.

'Miss Nude Australia,' I say out loud. I can't quite believe that this (previously) pudgy, pale redhead is actually Miss Nude Australia!

Winning was reassurance. *Yes, I am a good stripper after all.* I had got what I needed (a national title) in order to get what I wanted (international bookings and travel opportunities). With two big titles to my name, I was not just a stripper. I was, at last, a 'high-achieving' stripper.

Straight after Miss Nude was Miss Pole Dance Australia 2007. I only decided to enter a couple of weeks' prior. Nowadays, to enter a national-level pole competition, you need to dedicate yourself to a full-time training regime for at least three months beforehand. Not so in the early days of pole-dancing competitions. My mom helped me to cut up one of her old bras and, together, we studied Disney's *Snow White and the Seven Dwarves* so I could copy the poufy little arm sleeves. I felt like a kid again, doing a fun craft project with Mom.

In my routine, I was a wind-up doll who continually needed to spray her joints with WD-40 (a re-labelled can of hairspray, no way was lubricant going anywhere near a pole!) in order to keep pole dancing. I didn't place, but was awarded the title of 'Sponsor's Choice' and was thrilled to bits when they announced Ashleigh as the winner. Miss Nude and Miss Pole – we were the ultimate doubles team.

Too many adrenaline-filled adventures too close together and, finally, I crashed.

I got sick, really sick. Dad came over to take care of me. A customer had given me a video camera and Dad started playing with it, filming me on the couch.

'You've heard of Miss Nude?' he said, 'Well, this is Miss Sick!' before mixing me up some Gastrolyte.

He sat with me on the couch reading the paper and I sat quietly beside him, feeling sorry for myself but glad of his company. I thought back over the past few months. Something occurred to me.

'Dad,' I said, 'It's been four years since I've had a normal job. I'm not just surviving – I've actually got a thriving career going on!'

'Great. But what are you going to do next, Em?' he asked, looking over the top of his newspaper at me.

'Well, I'm really enjoying what I'm doing. I love getting up each day and going to work. What I love the most is that every day is slightly different. Sometimes I'm stripping, sometimes I'm teaching a pole class or an aerobics class … I guess I'll just ride this wave. Things seem to be going well and I should be able to get quite a bit of interstate and international travel off the Miss Nude title.'

'Sales!' he shouted back, excitedly.

I furrowed my brow in confusion. *Had he been listening to me at all?*

'You would be great at sales!' He flicked to the jobs section of the paper and started circling job ads for me.

'But Dad, I LOVE what I'm doing now. I love performing and teaching pole – I'm having a ball!'

He ignored me and continued circling jobs.

I was gutted. *I'm successful by my industry's standards … but not by his.*

I didn't tell him that *Penthouse Australia Magazine* had approached me about doing a cover and centerfold shoot. There are some things that a father does not need to know.

I was thrilled when the editor had called me – she said I would be doing a Rita Hayworth-inspired look, with a photographer who she knew and trusted. I was so excited that I was going to be a Penthouse Pet. I was eager to make a good impression so agreed to everything she said. We would be shooting at a brothel in – ironically named 'The Penthouse'.

I primed and primped and prepared for the shoot. Manicured, pedicured, spray tanned.

'Do you want a disposable G-string?' asked the tanner.

'Ummm … No. If I just bend over can you please have a really good look around down there and make sure all my cracks and crevices look okay?'

The tan was a bit of a disaster. The soles of my feet turned dark brown. I looked like I had stood in paint. Ashleigh tried to help me with exfoliant and a scrubbing brush, but I ended up wrapping sandpaper around her

TV remote and sanding the bottoms of my feet off. By the time I finished, my feet still looked slightly dirty, but at least not painted.

The morning of the shoot, Ashleigh carefully trimmed my pubic hair with a comb and scissors (that's what true friends do). I arrived early and made sure my phone was on silent. The make-up artist commented that my face 'takes make-up really well', which I thought meant she was worried when I walked in but felt better now that she'd waved her magic brushes over me.

Although the make-up went well, she struggled with my hair. Two hours in and she was still going. The photographer was impatient, 'Time's up – that'll have to do,' and we began shooting.

The shoot on the beach in Thailand with my 'cookie' out had been cheeky and fun. This was the complete opposite. The photographer decided I needed to look wet, turned on, glistening. He gave me some olive oil spray to apply to my pussy. I was a little unsure, but sprayed some on my palm and rubbed it on myself.

'More,' he said.

I hesitantly complied.

At that time, *Penthouse* released three different issues each month: *Penthouse*, *Penthouse Max* and the subscriber-only *Black Label* – each with an increasing level of explicitness. I was doing a solo shoot, to the level of 'open leg finger spread', for *Black Label*.

Glamour shoots are simple enough; you contort your body into uncomfortable, hyper-feminine shapes (butt out, boobs out). Close your eyes and open your mouth.

Snap, snap and voilà! It looks like you are orgasming on the page.

I cried when I saw my shoot.

The pictures were awful. Not because of what I was doing, but because they were bad – unflattering, ugly. My rushed hair and make-up, and the fact I didn't feel completely comfortable with the photographer, had been captured and published for all the world to see.

My mom comforted me. 'It will be gone in a month, Em, and people only really remember the cover shot anyway.'

I smiled at her through my red-rimmed eyes. This was the first time I felt real acceptance and understanding from her over my job.

Plus she was right – my cover did look hot!

I went into a few newsagents and stood near my magazine. I couldn't believe I was there on the cover. I wondered if anyone would recognise me. No one did. After hair, make-up and editing, the girl in the magazine didn't even look like the girl in the magazine.

Determined that this was not the way I would be immortalised in print, I agreed to a promo shoot for *The Picture* magazine – $200 to do a fully clothed, beer promotion. I figured I'd be dressed as some kind of beer wench, or sexy Oktoberfest/Heidi character. But when I arrived, it turned out I was to be dressed as a keg.

A keg.

With a little hat that I could pour beer from. I had to walk the streets and offer free beer to tradesmen. I did it, reckoning that it would be hilarious at least to share my day with the girls at work that night.

Ashleigh laughed uproariously when I told her. 'At least you weren't topless,' she said. 'The last one I did, I had my boobs out and they tried to convince me to hold a vibrator up and pretend to use it like a telephone.'

I shook my head. *Why did we do this?*

'Don't worry, it'll be off the shelves in a week. No one will see it.'

With her words echoing in my mind, I forgot all about it until a couple of months later when the shoot came out. There I was – a two-page spread, in all my kegged-out glory.

'Don't worry,' I told myself, 'no one will see it.'

Except that two of the other teachers at the pole school had their first glamour shoots in the same issue. Naturally, all the students bought copies and, a few pages after their gorgeous nude shoots, with make-up and hair-styling and beautiful lingerie and high heels, was me … in a keg.

Determined that *this* was not the way I was going to be immortalised in print, I flew to the coast for a full day of shooting with a new up-and-coming photographer. We were in a beautiful waterfront mansion and I had agreed to two days of shoots – trying to get through as many sets as possible. A set is a complete series of pictures, from dressed to naked, right up to whatever level of explicitness is required. It is then up to the photographer to try and sell the sets to the different magazines. But there's a catch.

If they don't sell, you don't get paid.

I was booked to do some basic glamour shoots and, on the second day, I would be doing a girl-girl shoot with

Phoenix Knight! I was so excited to see her again.

I posed in various stages of undress, in various locations around the beautiful home. It's a different kind of 'performance' to being naked onstage with hundreds of onlookers; there was only me, the photographer and the make-up artist. I felt glamorous and cared for. The photographer was polite and even cracked a few jokes. The make-up artist kept coming into the shoot to tuck in a tag, or sweep a stray hair behind my ear. She even held a straw for me to drink from so I didn't ruin my lipstick. It was fun – I felt like we were in our own little world, like the magic bubble I used to have in The Club. At least until some tradies started whooping and yelling at me when I posed outside on the balcony for a couple of shots.

After four different sets my back was aching – constantly sticking out your boobs and butt plays havoc with your lumbar – and I was so thankful I could relax in the pool overlooking the water that night. Here I was again in the luxury Richard lifestyle, without Richard, but still for work. I wondered if I would ever be able to afford this lifestyle for myself. I wondered if I wanted to. *Wasn't it better if other people were paying?*

I curled up in one of the giant king-sized beds and fell asleep Googling local property prices and mortgage calculators.

I was woken by sounds of activity in the other room. I came out to see the photographer arranging blue and pink dildos on the glass dining table I had been posing naked on the day before. My heart did a nervous beat.

'What are those for?' I asked. Phoenix and I were meant to be doing an R-rated shoot (nude, no open leg work).

'Not to worry,' the photographer said, cheerfully. 'I'm shooting some hard-core stuff with some other girls later this afternoon.'

I breathed a sigh of relief as Phoenix came bouncing through the door.

It was fun – she laughs while she shoots so her smiles look natural. I had a giant ingrown hair right beside my vagina, so was a little embarrassed and uncomfortable. I spent some time before each shot artfully arranging Phoenix's hands or hair to cover it, with her giggling all the while.

I had no idea if any of my sets would actually sell and was delighted to find out that two of my solos and my double with Phoenix would be appearing in upcoming issues of *The Picture* magazine. I didn't know when and it wasn't until I received a text message from a friend, saying they'd seen me naked in the latest issue at their local petrol station, that I hurried out to the nearest newsagency. I bought ten copies, which I could sign and sell at my Feature Shows. I flicked open to my 'spread' (pun intended), and stared in utter bewilderment and consternation at the page.

'That's not my vagina,' I mombled to myself. The magazine had airbrushed my natural 'outy' into a smooth bump with a single neat crease down the center.

The Picture magazine has an 'Unrestricted' rating. If you can see the inner labia, it changes the rating to

'Restricted'. Magazines classified as 'Restricted' (all open leg shots, or shots showing 'genital detail' or 'genital emphasis') must be sold in sealed plastic wrappers so kids can't randomly flick through the pages in a newsagency.

The erasure of all genital detail concerns me. I practically grew up in a strip club – I've been around naked women for most of my adult life. I know that pussies come in all sizes, shapes, colors and styles. But what if you're a young girl, who has only ever seen yourself naked, and all you can compare yourself to are the pictures in these magazines? Or what if you're a boy? I could potentially be the first naked girl you've ever seen and you're going to think anything outside of a 'designer vagina' is abnormal. There has been a rise in the popularity of labioplasty surgery (cutting off the outer parts of the inner labia) and it scares me to think that I might have contributed in some way to girls feeling abnormal. In all my years of being paid to be naked, I've learned that men really don't care about the size of your labia, your little pot belly or whether your boobs are big or small. You're naked. You have a vagina. They're happy.

I did many more glamour shoots over the ensuing years. Fetish shoots, bondage shoots, jeans porn (it's a thing), pictures of me getting my feet tickled and one nude shoot where I forgot my high heels and did two sets in my old converse sneakers. Some I was paid for; some I traded my time in return for copies of the shots.

Workers at one of my Dad's factories cut out and put up pictures of me from one of my *Picture* magazine shoots in the staff toilets, straining our already fractured relationship even further.

I decided to stop glamour modelling once I was in a committed, long-term relationship. The final shoot I had done was quite explicit – it was in *Picture Premium*, which comes in a plastic wrapper (Restricted rating). My boyfriend and I flicked through the pages of my exposed private parts together. My sex, my sexuality, so out there and on display. At least it wasn't airbrushed beyond recognition.

All the same, I said to him, 'I'm not sure I want to do shoots like this anymore.'

'That's good.'

I had done it. It was fun. But now it was time to move on to something else.

The magazines own the rights to those photos forever. Many of my shoots have been reprinted multiple times. I've even been topless in a 'spot the difference' game. Thankfully, the keg shots have never reappeared. Touch wood.

...

After my appearances in the magazines, especially *Penthouse*, my travel schedule began to pick up in intensity. I performed my first interstate Feature Shows. Arriving at the airport, I was met by a driver holding up a sign that stated 'Suzie Q'. He was incredibly disappointed that I wasn't Suzie Quatro and had no qualms telling me this as he drove me to the club where I would be performing.

Strip-club licensing is different from state to state and where I was headed permitted touching in the clubs. Ironically, it was also the only state where I could not sell my *Black Label Penthouse* magazines – they were considered 'too explicit'. In these 'touching clubs', customers are allowed to touch you above the waist only.

I was apprehensive. I had spent so many years drilling into my own head – as well as the customer's – 'Look, but don't touch'. I rebelled against the idea with every fibre of my being. The local dancers seemed unfazed (I guess it was normal to them) and so I attempted a few Private shows, holding the customer's hands tightly and grazing them along the sides of my breasts before twisting my body away, out of their reach. It didn't feel like a show. I didn't feel like I was performing. This was clearly crossing some line that I had within myself. I admitted that this was not for me, did my Feature Shows and went home.

I'm glad I tried – it firmed up my boundaries a little more. 'I will give you a lap dance, but I will not let you touch my breasts.' And I bet that some of those girls who worked there were okay with having their boobs touched by a stranger, but would not have been comfortable with an 'open leg, finger spread' shoot in a national magazine. We all have our own lines that we will not cross.

The secret is figuring out where your line is, then being strong enough to stick for it.

I had not crossed a boundary in doing my *Penthouse* shoot (although, in future I will always draw the line at cooking oil). I had simply learned that it was important to work with photographers I knew or had met previously. I was still excited and honoured to receive my 'key' (a beautiful gold necklace with the Penthouse logo) and to be part of the Penthouse Pet of the Year Awards.

I was hoping I would win. (What a trifecta: Erotic Star, Miss Nude Australia and Penthouse Pet of the Year!) I was visualising like crazy, even practicing my winning acceptance speech, just in case. 'I would like to dedicate this award to my parents, who, although not thrilled with my choice of career, have always remained quietly supportive. Thanks Mom and Dad.' I had my affirmation spelled out in letter magnets on my fridge: 'Pet of the Year'. I arrived early at the awards night and had my hair and make-up done – my hair was teased up into huge curls – 'The higher the hair, the closer to God, honey,' said the make-up artist, quoting Dolly Parton. I was given a sash with 'Penthouse Pet' written boldly in pink letters and I made my grand entrance out onto the floor of the club. I froze in the doorway as I stared at the milling throng of strangers. It was the same feeling of distress I had when it was time to quit The Club – *I don't know anyone. I can't talk to these people. The inane chit-chat, their incorrect assumptions and stupid questions* … I turned tail and headed back into the dressing room. Moments later, Ashleigh burst in and pulled me to my feet

'Ha!' she cried, 'I knew I would find you in here. Out. Now!'

I walked around the crowd, doing my best to mingle and socialise. The Suzie Switch seemed faulty and Ashleigh stood directly behind me, prodding me in the back and hissing 'smile' every few seconds. They lined us up to announce the winners. The usual blast of adrenaline began powering through my system. The announcement was made – I placed second. Which is okay. I seem to have broken my 'bridesmaid' spell with *Erotic Star* and Miss Nude.

The winner and I got booked to do a sexy double bath show for a late-night ad for sexy mobile phone downloads. The film crew asks if I will do a filming of an orgasm. A single shot of my face while I pretend to cum (like the website 'Beautiful Agony'). I decline. Again, there's that line between real sex and doing a sexy 'show'. From my diary:

> I'd rather show my vag than share an orgasm – even if it is a pretend one.

A few weeks later, Ashleigh and I were flown to Jakarta to pole dance in a five-star hotel at a magazine launch. The 'poles' are pieces of scaffolding screwed into a Perspex stage. We were told to spin clockwise only, as anticlockwise will undo the poles. The pipes are keening off at a weird angle and cracks are appearing in the Perspex as we dance. My motto for surviving as a performer? *Just cope.*

A drag queen called Claire De Lune was performing with us as well. She says she usually has male back-up dancers for her final set and can we please put on suits and learn her choreography? So here are we girls, dressed as boys, back-up dancing for a man dressed as woman – who's removing his make-up and outfit live onstage to become a man again.

Once we were back, I learned that the gender-fluid performer's real name was Marc. He had just become the manager of a bar/restaurant on Oxford St called Slide. He was interested in purchasing a pole and booking pole dancers there; could I help him?

I jumped at the chance. I sold him a pole and started to book dancers there for weekly pole spots – pole shows! Where you didn't have to take your clothes off? The dancers were also paid – and I earned a small commission. I met Marc's actual back-up dancers, James and Paul, who asked me for pole lessons so they could do some of the pole numbers at Slide.

During their first lesson, I taught them a couple of beginner moves and they dropped into perfect splits on the floor. I nodded, 'Yeah – I think you'll be fine at this.'

I believe they were the first professional male pole dancers in Australia. They named themselves the 'Aussie Pole Boys'. I introduced them to Ashleigh. Together, the four of us formed 'The Aussie Pole Stars'. We performed together at some of the big gay and lesbian parties, at a club in Noumea and at complex group shows for Hellfire. One particularly memorable show was for the inaugural 'Hellfire Afloat' – essentially, putting the club night onto a boat and cruising around the harbour, where we performed a kinky massacred version of the fairy tale *Peter Pan*. The two boys were Peter Pants and Captain Cock. Ashleigh and I were Bendy Wendy and Kinkabelle. There was drug taking (What else do you think 'pixie dust' is?), lap dancing, double-double pole and an acrobatic orgy sequence. I asked my non-industry partner what he thought of the whole thing.

'I like to think of it as art,' he replied.

Nice.

I'm not sure coke-fuelled orgies dressed as children's fairy tale characters is high-brow art, but I truly appreciated this first-ever show of support from my significant other for my career.

The four of us began performing at a new show night Marc had launched at Slide called 'El Circo' – a nine-course degustation menu of nine circus acts. I had my Lyra and pole skills, and the boys had put together their own duo pole act – Marc also booked magicians, jugglers and even a male belly dancer.

I was slipping further and further away from my life as a stripper. I was hired as Rebecca's assistant to help audition and train the new girls – now I was the one breaking people's dreams, telling them they were too overweight to be a stripper. There was a kind of checklist: pretty face, hot body, good dancer and nice personality. They could have a black mark in one, or maybe two, of those columns, but not all four. I liked to think I was helping create the 'next generation' of baby strippers, encouraging them to save their money and not get too caught up in the drinking and partying. I hope they listened.

Gayna, my mentor and Stripper Queen, had fully moved out of the 'worker' side of the industry; she had become the Dancer Manager for a club. When she offered to fly me up to do Features for her, I jumped at the chance. But it was not fun. After someone declined a Private Show with me because 'for the same price (he) could get two bags of pilchers' (fish bait), I found I just couldn't muster up enough enthusiasm to get out and work the floor. The Suzie Switch was broken. I just didn't care anymore.

I felt ungrateful. I had this amazing title – this should have been the zenith of my stripping career – but I was over it. I vowed, 'No more strip clubs.' It was no longer fun. It was tiring. I didn't want to talk to men anymore and pander to whatever their wishes were; I wanted to 'independ' rather than depend on men for my success.

I focused more on my pole-teaching career, teaching several group classes a week as well as multiple private lessons. With the income I was pulling in from my seven days/seven nights a week work schedule, plus the added cash injection from winning Miss Nude, I had enough cash to stump up a deposit on an investment property. 'Property millionaire. Retire by thirty.' was my mantra, the spell I cast over my life. My dad was a successful entrepreneur, owning and operating multiple businesses he'd started from scratch. I still had this subconscious need for his approval. For him to be proud of me. All my pole and stripping success had failed to impress him (not surprisingly) and our relationship was still strained from my *Picture* shoot being plastered up in his staff toilets. Our conversations still skirted any topic that remotely related to my career. Once I had decided to open my own pole-dancing school, we suddenly had some common ground. From having nothing to talk about, we now could now discuss contractors, council regulations and management styles. Opening my own business was the first step in healing the rift in our relationship.

Chapter 9

I'm not a Stripper ... I'm a Pole Dancer (I'm also a Stripper)

I am 26 years old.

Charlee was one of my pole students, an ambitious business woman with three children, who began private lessons with me in order to master some moves she was finding difficult. We hit it off immediately and our chats ranged from our backgrounds (she had previously owned a real-estate agency and graphic design company) to the stripping industry (she enjoyed hearing the tales of my naked hijinks). One day, our conversation turned to the idea of opening a pole studio together. I asked her what her goals were.

She said, 'Build a successful business.'

I said, 'I want to be a property millionaire and retire by thirty.'

We didn't really know each other that well but, upon discovering we had the same birthday, we took it as 'a sign' that we were destined to become business partners.

I was nervous about starting my own business, scared that it wouldn't work out. I hadn't burned any bridges in the stripping industry so I could go back any time I wanted to, but I didn't really want to. I had even been turned off the 'Madame' idea – after working as Rebecca's assistant, I had learned that few girls saw stripping as a career, as I did. Most did not. They would frequently run late for shifts, break the rules or sometimes just not show up to work at all. I reassured myself that I was a hard worker and, if all else failed, then I could always go and work at McDonald's. It sounds like I am being funny, but this thought was actually quite reassuring.

The first official business meeting for Suzie Q Pole Studio (SQPS) took place in a swingers' club, where I was performing a strip show. Between Charlee managing her household and her kids, and my work schedule, the only time we were both free to meet was 11 p.m. on a Saturday night! The bulk of our business meetings ended up taking place over phone and email. We signed the lease on a space above an Italian restaurant. Our students had to walk through the restaurant to enter the studio upstairs and we shared bathrooms with the restaurant's patrons. We bought our girls little pink 'modesty robes' to cover their pole outfits. Charlee's husband and his builder mates installed twenty-four gleaming brass 38 mm spinning poles, and Charlee and I painted 'WE WILL ROCK THIS' in big capital letters behind the mirrors. Our secret promise to each other.

Charlee filled our first two Beginners pole classes by waiting outside the local train station, thrusting fliers into the hands of any woman aged between 18 and 50. Her sales skills were, and still are, awe-inspiring. One day, she stepped out to buy us coffees and came back with a list of seven new sign-ups. I wished she'd been a hostess in The Club – I would have been booked solidly in Privates!

Our students were an eclectic mix of ages, backgrounds and careers. Nurses, teachers, moms (and sometimes their daughters) and we even had a police hostage negotiator, who left her pager beside me on the stage each class 'just in case'. I was working as a personal trainer and fitness instructor, even doing a stint on the TV show *Aerobics Oz Style*, and I blended my fitness-industry knowledge with my exotic-dance background to create a syllabus and routines that were fun, cheeky and provided a balanced total body workout. Our students would be trying so hard to master a new move they didn't notice they had done about twenty reps of lifting their body weight. The changes in their body shapes came quickly – plus, I think they found pole to be a lot more fun than the gym (and our pink lighting was a lot more flattering). Women flocked to us in droves as a genuine fitness alternative.

This presented us with a problem: I couldn't physically teach so many classes. We had to hire staff. In 2008, you couldn't just post a 'Pole Instructor Wanted' ad (although I reckon you could now) and so we recruited my friends, people I liked, who I wanted to work with. Some of them were strippers so I taught them about anatomy and safe exercise design. Some of them were fitness instructors so I encouraged them to move in a softer, more sensual way. Each of them was beautiful and brought their own unique talents to the studio, but each was also human.

'Why can't they vacuum properly?' Charlee grumbled to me. 'I already clean up after three kids.'

In that moment, staring at each other across a tangled vacuum cord, I think we both realised no one would ever love Suzie Q Pole Studio as much as we did.

It was hard watching those first few classes, watching someone else teach my material, my choreography. 'That's not how I would have done that.' But I had to learn to trust my staff. Gradually, I let go of my need to control everything in the classes at the studio.

Sort of.

I would sit up the back and make notes on where the teacher could improve.

After all, you can always be better, right?

The SQPS Team was exactly that, a team. We walked around in matching shirts that said 'Suzie Q Pole Studio' on the front and 'Nobody Knows I'm a Pole Dancer' in hot pink letters on the back. Charlee may have had three kids already, but through the studio she gained over a hundred more. She was like a mother hen to all of us. She knew every student by name and a few facts about them (again, she would have been great in a strip club). If the students were her babies, then the staff were mine. I tried my best to coach, train and support them in their own burgeoning careers, as they won amateur and professional pole titles. One of them even won Miss Nude Australia!

I felt like I had figured out the formula for winning competitions. Get the judging criteria. Memorise it. Meet it.

For some reason though, I refused to apply this logic to my own Miss Pole Dance Australia preparations. The criteria is simple:

Pole Tricks – 15 points

Dance – 10 points

Presentation/show – 5 points

Year after year, I put very little time into training and mastering new tricks. The truth was, I hated competing. I just wanted to perform, to do a good show, to entertain people. I got nervous when I performed, but that was nothing compared to heart-palpitating, sickening sense of dread I felt before a competition. My hands sweated (fatal when you're about to rely on them to grip a slippery metal tube), my breath ran short and fast, and my heart raced at a million miles a minute. Busting out my show as planned was only half the battle. The other half was keeping my adrenaline and nerves at a manageable level.

Four members of the SQPS Team competed in Miss Pole Dance Australia in 2008. We trained together (drank tea and champagne and, occasionally, did some pole). We were competitors, but we were also each other's coaches, critics and support network.

'Suzie Q' became bigger than just me. When I stepped out onstage, I was no longer just representing myself, but also Charlee, my studio, my staff and my students. I needed to be good.

I decided I had better go train some tricks.

I began to attend regular yoga classes to increase my flexibility and adult gymnastics classes to learn some new skills for Miss Pole Dance. An added bonus of the gymnastics class was that there were a couple of attractive guys – I smiled and introduced myself. It turned out *Best Undressed* had been on television the night before. They already knew who I was and they had already seen me naked.

'It must be really hard for you to find a boyfriend,' commented one.

Goddamn it, it was the cute one – why did the cute one turn out to be a dickhead?

I politely pointed out to Toby (his name) that I was only friends with people who had no issue with what I did.

I did not point out that we would therefore never be friends.

But I thought it.

I thought it very hard.

Such a dickhead.

I really didn't have time for people like that in my life, anyway. Pole had begun to explode in popularity around the world. It grew and evolved so fast. New moves were being created all the time. I was kept busy at the studio, inventing more levels, new syllabuses and new routines. Trying to keep our material fresh and 'cutting edge'.

Students joined us from other pole schools. I was distressed when they said, 'Oh I can't do that trick on my left side.' Their previous school had taught them tricks using their right arm.

Using *only* their right arm.

'What?! Do you go to the gym and do bicep curls with only your left arm?' I asked.

'Of course,' piped up Ashleigh, who had come to

teach for me at SQPS, 'I need to balance out all that pole on my right side.'

Ashleigh, always the smart-ass.

Students raced through each level, eager for more. Moves that took Ashleigh and I weeks to create and master were picked up in a couple of lessons – the difference between having a good teacher and having to figure things out for yourself. Our own personal pole practice became more and more important – to keep ahead of our students, ahead of the industry. Students wanted to learn the next hardest move. The next trick. They barely mastered one before looking to the next. I had to keep telling them to slow down or they would get injured. Trying to keep them safe. A girl in the UK became a paraplegic after falling from a pole. This sickened me. I created 'Tests' that my students had to master before they could move up a level – ensuring they were not only strong enough to execute a move, but also strong enough to exit safely. I felt personally responsible for the safety and well-being of these women. I was a hard taskmaster. In everything I ever did, I wanted to be good. Better. The best. I assumed my students wanted the same. I reduced some girls to tears by yelling at them: 'Point your fucking toes. Seriously. It's hurting my face to look at you.' I had been coached a similar way in gymnastics and didn't really embrace any kind of love other than 'tough'.

People seemed to like it though and, thanks to Charlee, we had a steady stream of would-be polers flocking to us. I tried to help her with marketing and promotion, handing out fliers on a busy street.

'Hi there, have you ever thought about trying pole dancing?'

'Oh, I could never do that, I don't want to be a stripper.'

'No worries! There are no strippers here. This is a certified stripper-free zone!'

I smiled weakly and left Charlee to handle the general public. I isolated myself away from a judgemental society, who doesn't understand, doesn't 'get it', and surrounded myself with my staff and students, who understand the magic of this place. The magic of pole.

We were the only pole school out in Western Sydney and our classes were popular. Really popular. We moved to a bigger warehouse space, where we offered circus classes as well. The added bonus was that we no longer had to worry about tottering through a busy Italian restaurant in hot pants and six-inch heels.

The local primary school protested against our business application, concerned about the effect of our signage would have on the students. Charlee and I wrote a measured and thought-out response to council:

> Although we appreciate the concerns raised by our would-be neighbours, we would like to reassure them that we are located at the end of a quiet cul-de-sac with an innocuous sign and the only way the local school children would be exposed to our business would be if they were trespassing through the industrial area at night or on the weekend (our classes only operate well outside of school hours).

Chapter 9

We were approved.

The extra space meant we now had room for more students. We began an ambitious marketing campaign. Not just to recruit new girls, but also to educate the general public about what pole dancing really was.

We did a pole display in the shop window of a women's fitness clothing store in the local shopping center. We wore sneakers, running shorts and singlets. I forbade the girls from doing body rolls, booty shaking or any other 'sexy' movements.

Center Management fielded a number of complaints about our 'inappropriate display' from disgruntled customers.

I firmly believe we could have executed the same moves, in the same outfits, in the same way, on a piece of fabric, and there would have been no complaints.

Sure enough, when we did an aerial yoga display a few months later – same outfits, legs spread apart, upside down in an aerial yoga hammock, no one batted an eyelid. No complaints at all.

What is it about pole that makes it so offensive to people? Pole dancing in a pole studio is very different to pole dancing in a strip club. I don't think I've ever seen anything less sexy than a bunch of beginner polers attempting a body roll for the first time (apologies, beginner girls). There is nothing inherently offensive about being upside down in a pair of shorts, it all comes down to the meaning that people ascribe to the act.

As pole classes grew in popularity, so did pole shows. People wanted pole dancers to perform at their events, Christmas parties and birthdays. Not strippers. Pole dancers. Ashleigh and I were booked to perform three pole numbers at a corporate Christmas party at the Museum of Contemporary Art. We rehearsed for weeks, making sure our kicks, tricks and hair flicks were perfectly synchronised. But we were asked to leave after just one number. The women at the party found us insulting. Really, I think a lot of it is just semantics. Tell a woman to come to a 'strip show' or watch a 'pole dancer' and she'll wrinkle her nose in disgust. Give her the exact same performance, but call it 'Burlesque', and you'll get a completely different reaction.

Another time, I was booked to be a 'Live Mannequin' in the shop window of an upmarket lingerie boutique. Most people smiled as I waved at them with my brightly colored ostrich feather fans. But one young mother furiously berated the store manager for allowing such a 'disgusting display' to be seen by her toddler. She looked over at my stricken face and said, 'I'm sorry, I'm sure you're very lovely. But my kid doesn't need to see,' she gestured vaguely towards my body, 'that'.

I looked down at myself. I was wearing more than most people wore to the beach. I wasn't doing anything overtly sexual – in fact, most of my body was obscured by the large feathered fans I was holding.

Why are people so angered by things they perceive as 'sex', which aren't actually sex at all. She'd clearly had sex fairly recently, judging from the baby in the pram and the toddler hanging off her hand. Presumably her toddler wasn't offended. What was she trying to protect him from?

Charlee and I gave up on shop windows altogether. We took our marketing displays somewhere they couldn't possibly cause offence.

We booked a stand at Sexpo.

Sexpo is the county fair of the adult industry. This travelling carnal carnival moves around the capital cities annually. Brightly colored dildos festoon the stands, alongside blow-up dolls and inflatable sheep. Show bags with lingerie, lube and condoms are sold by hawkers shouting, 'Get your butt plugs here!' There are displays of flogging, rope bondage and even a mini strip club, where you can get a lap dance from a real live stripper. There is a bucking bull (shaped like a penis), a ghost train (also shaped like a penis) and men walking around in inflatable mascot suits (yup, they're penises, too, lovingly referred to as 'Penisaurus' and 'Cock Man'). The artist 'Pricasso' paints people's portraits using his penis as a brush. There are pole dancing displays, male strippers, female strippers and famous porn stars signing autographs for adoring fans.

We were trying to move pole dancing away from the sex industry, to make it more palatable for mainstream women. But the sex industry was the only industry that would actually support us.

Sexpo runs for four days and the days are long. You start at 10 a.m. and work through until the show closes at midnight each night. You had to be enthusiastic and having fun. It was like a really long table-dancing shift. At the end of four days, everyone was exhausted. My feet were blistered and bleeding, one of the porn stars was asleep under her signing table and Pricasso was soaking his member in a mixture of Dettol and warm water.

It was, however, a fantastic way to recruit new students and, as an added bonus, I was asked to be part of the Sexpo Crew as a Feature Showgirl and their female emcee.

Sexpo was my first job emcee-ing anything and it was petrifying. Tell me to get onstage and get completely naked in front of thousands of people and I barely bat an eyelid. Place a microphone in my hand and I break out in a cold sweat. I still loved public speaking, but it made me nervous as hell.

However, stripping was something I knew intimately and it's easy to talk about something when you know it and love it. A strip show emcee has to whip the crowd into a maddening frenzy of yells, cheers, whoops and whistles – 'Do you like what you see here? D'ya wanna see MOOOORRREE!!!?! Because the louder you cheer, the quicker those clothes come off!'

This is a blatant lie, of course.

The performers are performing a choreographed routine. Their pants are going to come off during a crescendo in the last song. Every time. Regardless of how loudly you yell.

I personally have never liked an emcee spruiking during my shows. I once had a judge pull me aside at a stripping competition and say he really respected the fact I hadn't 'asked' for applause (cupping my hand around my ear in an 'I can't hear you?' type of gesture). I took that compliment to heart and made it one of my principles to never, ever ask for applause – 'If they're not clapping, you're not good enough.'

I loved performing at Sexpo. The audience was an equal mix of men and women, and the women responded just as positively to my shows as the men. They appreciated my skills on the pole and the fact I was being sensual without being overly sexual. I hoped that by seeing me perform, and actually enjoying the show, they would be a little less quick to pass judgement on strippers in the future.

In between juggling my classes at the studio, shows at the pubs and clubs, and hiring girls for The Club, my Dad rang me to ask when we could catch up.

I started singing 'Cats in the Cradle': 'She'd grown up just like me, my girl was just like me,' down the phone to him and explained. I really couldn't – I was trying to squeeze in as much training as possible for Miss Pole Dance. I was up against Felix Cane. The woman was super-talented, super-sexy and practically superhuman. I knew I couldn't beat her, but hoped to perform a memorable show and at least come in second place.

'Well, if that's the only way I'm going to see you, I had better come to that competition then.'

I almost dropped the phone in shock. *My dad, coming to see me pole dance? Coming to support me in my pole career?* He had never seen me perform before. I doubled my training efforts. I not only wanted to do a good job for myself, my career and my studio now. I desperately wanted to impress him. I wanted to make him proud.

I took my preparations and training more seriously

than ever before. I chose to do a 'Mission Impossible' themed show, and enlisted the help of a choreographer and professional costume designer (I wasn't going to be wearing one of Mom's old bras this time). I demanded a 'full body catsuit like the movie. Except that my arms, legs and torso need to be exposed so I can grip onto the pole.' Fabric slips, skin grips – skimpy outfits are 'de rigueur' for pole. And, somehow, he delivered.

I didn't sleep at all the night before. But my show went well! I placed second to Felix, just as I'd hoped and I heard those magic words from Dad:

'Good job, Em.'

I was so grateful that he finally came to see me perform. I was even more delighted to learn my second placing still qualified me for Miss Pole Dance World! I could be representing the country … in pole dancing!

An email arrived from the organiser of Miss Pole Dance World. My post-comp high slammed back down to Earth. He described me hosting Sexpo as a 'big problem' and I that I could not expect his organisation to 'defend these kinds of activities'.

I cried hot tears of frustration. I never asked him to defend anything. I'd spent years trying to normalise the marginalised stripping industry, explaining over and over that it was a job, just a job. Trying to explain to non-industry friends that I was a stripper … but it was really cool because I got paid to travel the world doing what I loved. There was no point really; they had tapped out of the conversation at 'stripper'.

Now I found myself doing the same thing in the

equally marginalised and misunderstood world of pole dancing. Only this time I was being thwarted by someone who was purportedly on the same side as me!

The organiser informed me that there would be a €25,000 fine if the winner of MPD World associated herself with the sex industry in any way. He wanted pole to be recognised as an Olympic sport. He's not the only one. People who want pole to be taken seriously are keen to disassociate it from its strip-club roots – focusing instead on its links with the more acrobatic Mallakhamba and Chinese Pole. There is a growing dichotomy within the industry between *Pole Dance* and *Pole Fitness*. I fully support pole dancing's Olympic bid, but it would sadden me to see it reduced entirely to a sport, with no show, no story. I would like to see room for both, for people able to pole dance in their own way, whatever that might be.

For me, I love pole dancing because I am an entertainer and I still believe 'people are there to be entertained.'

The final nail in the coffin for me was that he wanted me to compete under my real name. I scoffed at this: *Why on Earth would I do that? No one knows who Emma is.*

Not even me.

Another national pole comp was released. The rules stated that you cannot enter if you are 'a stripper, have ever been a stripper, or associate with strippers.'

I wanted to give up. Do they think I'll get disoriented by the lights and poles, and start taking my clothes off and rubbing my breasts?

Don't get me wrong, I like that I am a stripper; I am proud of being a stripper.

But I am not a stripper all the time. I am fully capable of keeping my clothes on while performing onstage.

Thankfully, it was not just me who was put out by the rules. There was uproar in the pole community – many, if not all, of the pioneers in the pole industry were strippers. Yes, pole dancing has been influenced by the circus arts, but also by burlesque dancers swinging around tent poles in travelling carnivals. It was strippers like Fawnia Mondey, who opened the world's first-ever dedicated pole studio in Canada in the late 1990s, and Bobbi, who opened Australia's first pole studio in 2003, who brought pole dancing out of the strip clubs and made it accessible to the general public in the first place.

By all means sanitise it. Segregate it from stripping. But please do not forget or insult the first wave of polers, who bore the brunt of society's criticisms to make way for this sport and art form.

From the outside, my life was glittering. I was flown around the world to teach and perform. That five-star lifestyle, introduced to me by Richard, was now my own. The fancy hotels now paid for by me or, at least, by whoever was booking me. But the truth is, I was lonely.

Ashleigh and I booked a holiday in tropical Thailand but I couldn't relax. I was thinking about work and choreographing routines for the pole studio. While we were in Thailand, Charlee called. She was organising life-insurance policies for us both and wanted to know who she should put as my beneficiary. She has nominated her children. *I have a pet rat; can you nominate a rat?*

I asked her what I should do.

She paused. 'Yeah, ummm…' she trailed off awkwardly.

I felt very alone. I told her to just put my mom.

The cute boy from gymnastics, Toby, was right. It really is hard to find a boyfriend when you work as a stripper.

Or pole dancer.

Or both.

I complained to Ashleigh, 'I'll never find someone who loves me for me, who accepts what I do.'

'You're going to have to date in-industry, babe. That's the only way you're going to find someone who is okay with what you do.'

I flew home from Thailand early. I didn't like sitting around all day. I actually preferred to be working. At that time, if I had been diagnosed with a fatal disease I would have still done my shows and taught my classes; there was actually nothing I would have preferred to do. On the flight home, my mind drifted to my 'in-industry' options. Recalling the bulked-up male strippers from Sexpo, with their piles of pre-workout and protein powders, I felt even more alone and depressed. I didn't want to date 'in industry'.

But what if I met someone and then brought him into the industry …?

Turns out he was under my nose the whole time.

Chapter 10

Toby J. The Beginning

I am 27 to 29 years old.

I was still going to both yoga and adult gymnastics even after Miss Pole Dance, because I enjoyed the cross-training for pole. I know the name 'Adult Gymnastics' makes it sound exciting – especially considering my colorful career so far – but really it's just a gymnastics class for grown-ups rather than kids. Some of the people at adult gym (including the cute dickhead, Toby) were into acro – a form of gymnastics with two people, where the 'base' balances the 'flyer'. I began to try out a few skills with them. I enjoyed being a flyer, held up by a strong (and often attractive) man, in whom I had to put all my faith and trust. It felt freeing, a letting-go of the control that I fought so hard to maintain in my everyday life. All I had to do was hold my body tight and trust. I didn't have to do so much, try so hard. I was enjoying training acro so much, I decided to try and put it into a performance.

It seems to be my modus operandi. Take something I love – whether it's pole dancing, fitness or performing

– then figure out a way, not to monetise it necessarily, but to at least make it self-sustaining, so I can do it more often. Do it more often and call it 'work'. Because for me, when it's 'work' it's okay to prioritise it above all else.

I needed a goal, something to work towards with my acro training and so I decided to put together a performance for an event Charlee and I were running, called PoleCandy. We'd noticed there weren't many opportunities for up-and-coming pole dancers to perform in Sydney. And just like me, having something to work towards is important for all pole dancers – be it an event, competition or show, it forces you to step up your training and really hone your skills. PoleCandy was an amateur pole comp that we created to give budding performers the chance to clock up some extra stage time. I also figured it would be an opportunity for me to put my burgeoning emcee skills into practice. I approached one of the guys at training who seemed to know what he was doing. He also happened to have a particularly nice body.

'I've got this amateur pole event thing coming up – would you be willing to do a show with me?'

He agreed and we began training. Toby-the-cute-dickhead actually helped us out by coaching us through some of the moves. I slowly forgave the cute American for his earlier comments about it being hard to find a boyfriend. As we became closer, and I began to feel more comfortable around him, I felt the need to bring it up again.

'You know what you said when you met me, about it

being hard to find a boyfriend? I'm actually really careful about who I choose to spend time with. I simply don't spend time with people like that – people who have a problem with what I do.'

'Yes, but I grew up on a dairy farm in rural Wisconsin, Midwest America. The guys out there wouldn't even let me *speak* to their girlfriends, so I just couldn't imagine how someone would cope with your career. I'm sorry if I offended you, but I really was simply curious.'

He had touched a raw nerve. I'd had several relationships blow up and end because of my job. I'd started to believe it really was difficult, if not impossible, for me to find a boyfriend.

I accepted his apology and threw myself into training. The problem was – Mr Nice Body was ridiculously unreliable. I'd never had to rely on a partner before. If a show didn't go well, if I hadn't rehearsed enough, I could only blame myself. Now I was being faced with increasingly creative excuses as to why he couldn't make training each week.

'I didn't bring training clothes with me.'

'I forgot.'

'*Underbelly* was on TV.'

'My belt hurt my back today.'

I began to share these excuses with 'Coach Toby' each week. We'd laugh together then he'd fill in and base me. Eventually, PoleCandy was only a couple of weeks away. I asked the original partner to step down and Toby to step in. Toby was a National Sports Acrobatic champion, but he'd never previously performed. I helped him with his 'show face' and he helped me with the actual acro skills.

As the date of our first performance drew closer, we stepped up our rehearsal schedule. Toby began to skip work to come into the pole school to train with me during the day. We talked and laughed as we failed skills and collapsed in a tangle of limbs. Our interactions began to border on flirting. I trained in my cotton Target underwear with sassy slogans written across the backside and when Toby held me in various positions he could 'read what message your butt holds for me today.' We went out for dinner or ice cream after our training sessions and I found myself growing increasingly attracted to him.

I started to become acutely aware of his body as he was holding mine. I had to trust him completely as he held me above his head with one arm and I'd always wrap my arms around him in a huge hug after each training session, grateful for his strength and his care of me. These post-training hugs grew longer and longer until our final rehearsal, the day of PoleCandy, when he kissed me.

As he pulled his lips from mine, he asked, 'What are we?'

I was completely stressed out about running the event. I shook my head and begged him, 'Ask me later, please!'

I was right to be stressed; the pole we were using fell down during rehearsals. Toby stepped in, figured out how it worked and fixed it. He could always fix anything, do anything. I nicknamed him 'MacGyver'. Our first performance together went smoothly. Many people commented on the chemistry apparent between us onstage.

He pulled me aside again a few days later. Again he asked, 'What are we?'

I stared back at him, helplessly. Toby was an adventure camping tour guide. He spent most of his life living out of a backpack, sleeping under the stars, and he used shampoo as face wash. He was very, very different to anyone I'd ever dated before. I was used to dating 'metrosexual'-type guys – who co-ordinated their ties and cufflinks and could be counted on to loan me an exfoliant if I'd forgotten mine. Toby had an excessive amount of body hair and didn't own a pair of shoes. He came to collect me at The Club after a Feature Show one night and had to buy shoes especially so he would comply with the dress code and be allowed in. He complained at how expensive food was when we went out to eat. This was a far cry from previous dates, one of whom had cried out, 'Let's eat like millionaires tonight!' and dropped $700 on a meal with me.

I couldn't quite get my head around the idea of a long-term life with him – no dressing up, no fancy restaurants, no cocktail bars (he didn't drink). Thanks to Richard and a slew of other well-off boyfriends, I was used to being collected from the airport in a limo with a glass of champagne waiting for me. Now it was Toby's furry smiling face in a beat-up old Hyundai. As we spent more and more time together, I begin to question which lifestyle I actually preferred. It's all very well eating a $700 meal when it's someone else's money, but when it's 'our' money?

We discovered that we both trained at the same circus center. He would have been up above me on the flying trapeze while I trained below on my aerial hoop for Miss

Nude Australia – but we had somehow never bumped into each other.

Our circus coach suggested we try double trapeze together. Toby was, and is, such an amazing base that I had no issue trusting him completely as he quite literally held my life in his hands (or off one foot) six metres in the air. I felt a bit like Jane being thrown around by Tarzan. Our twice-weekly training sessions were followed by dinner dates and romantic walks.

He brought up the idea of living together.

We'd only been seeing each other for a couple of months – but I already felt like I wanted to tie up my life with his. I subscribe to the school of thought that says 'pressure cook your relationships'. Move in. Go through something stressful. Test the relationship. If it survives, you've got yourself a keeper. If it doesn't, well, that just saved you a whole heap of time – it could have taken months, even years of 'just seeing each other' to figure out you don't work well as a team. Toby moved in to my little one-bedroom apartment and we started our relationship.

Except, we didn't.

He was still leading camping tours; I was still travelling for stripping and for pole. Due to our conflicting travel schedules, for the first twelve months of being 'together' we were apart more than were actually together.

'Dammit, these things are hard,' he said, as he wrestled with two pairs of six-inch heels, trying to get them to fit together like a jigsaw. He was helping me pack for a tour of the UK and Paris.

Chapter 10

While I was there, the Manager of X-Pole (a big international pole company) suggested coming back for a couple of months next year – there was the possibility of bringing Toby with me. A little seed of an idea started to take root in my mind … *Travelling the world, teaching pole, with the love of my life by my side? Yes, please!*

When I returned, he'd already left for a gymnastics display team tour of Denmark and the UK. I opened the door to our little home and found that, not only had he hired a steam cleaner and cleaned the carpets, he'd stocked the freezer with four different types of ice cream and had somehow taught himself to crochet – he'd re-crocheted an unravelling jumper while I was gone. MacGyver indeed. I made him a card with a crossed-out chameleon on the front and wrote *Don't go changin'* on the inside.

I loved him, just as he was.

While he was away, I judged a state competition of Miss Pole Dance. I was blown away by 'Ministry of Pole' – a new doubles team that revolutionised doubles pole. Traditionally, doubles pole consists of two girls doing synchronised moves on two separate poles. Ministry of Pole were doing double-trapeze moves, with a base and flyer – two girls on one pole, with one holding the other's entire body weight. Their routine resembled the double-trapeze routine that Toby and I had been working on. I sent Toby a text, telling him it was time to 'get his furry butt on the pole.'

When we were apart, I missed him. He was a genuinely gorgeous person – both outside and in. I got the feeling he was one of those once-in-a-lifetime opportunities that made all the shitty waiting around for each other worth it. Even my insomnia was eased with his arms wrapped around me as I slept. He was a safe haven for me, a soothing presence for my stressed-out mind.

People used to tell me all the time, 'Wow, you get to travel so much! That's so glamorous and exciting.' I wanted to tell them to try taking thirty days off from their partner and their life at a time, with only a few days respite in between. My trips were back-to-back and I was so caught up planning the 'next thing', I never took the time to enjoy 'this thing'. It was exciting, but I didn't give myself enough time to appreciate it. Toby led one final adventure tour up the east coast and, when he returned, we came to an agreement – no more major trips without each other. I wanted him to quit his job and become my manager. Ashleigh had said the only way I'd find a boyfriend comfortable with what I did was to date 'in-industry'. Here was my alternative to dating 'in-industry'.

Find the perfect man and bring him *into* the industry.

The Asia-Pacific Pole Championships announced that, for the first time, they were allowing mixed pairs in their competition. They were already trailblazers by being the first pole competition in the world to include a Men's Division. Still on a mission to secure myself a national title in pole dancing, I instantly thought of teaming myself up with the previous year's Men's Division winner. But Toby was having none of it.

'No.'

'But why not?'

'You're my partner now.'

'But you can't pole dance.'

'I'll learn.'

I brought him into the studio to help me teach an advanced pole class. I was nervous about how the girls would react to having a man in the class. But they loved him – referring to him as 'Mr Suzie'. After class, when the studio was closed for the night, we began his pole training. We skipped all the beginner moves – I got him in his underwear and upside down on the pole straight away.

'Okay, you've got yourself up there. Now hold me as well.'

'Fuck off. I'm getting down now.'

'Maybe you should shave your legs?'

'Yes! Wrapping my legs around a metal tube is painful enough. I'm also dealing with having my leg hairs ripped out one by one.'

A few days later, he texted me a picture of his freshly shaven legs with the words 'See what I'm willing to do for you.'

'Show me one where you're upside down on a pole,' I texted back.

He replied with a series of unhappy emojis.

Although initially worried that I was sacrificing my 'lifestyle' for Toby, I realised that our lifestyle was actually awesome. We'd wake up and cook breakfast together – scromlettes (when an omelette fails and kind of becomes scrambled eggs), go to our respective jobs for the day, meet up at the Circus Center to train, then cook dinner together when we got home. It was wonderful and magical. These were the golden times. Everything we did together was fun. We wrestled in the middle of training, sang 80s cartoon themes and made dog and cat noises at each other. We would stay up late at night, decorating hula hoops and singing country-and-western songs. We were busy but we didn't mind; we were together. Permeating our idyllic love bubble, however, was a growing sense of nervousness from me. Our first-ever aerial performance was drawing closer. I had begun booking Toby on my performance bookings.

'I know you just wanted me but, for a slight increase in price, you can have two of us!'

My clients were booking him purely based on my word and I felt like the name and reputation of 'Suzie Q' was at stake. I wanted us to be good. Not just good, better than good. Toby would say, 'we are good enough,' and I would reply, 'Good enough is not *good enough*.' I had this fantasy of us performing and travelling together for a living. The only way to achieve that was to strive for absolute excellence or, even better, perfection. The only way to achieve perfection was work.

Lots and lots of hard work.

Our first trapeze show together was at Sexpo. I sprained a muscle in my back the day before and was crying on the floor right before we were due to go on. Toby stroked my hair and told me I'd be okay, that 'adrenaline and love' would get me through. 'Adrenaline and love' became our private catchphrase; we chanted it to each other before every show from that time on. He was right, of course. The show went off without a hitch. People loved it, Sexpo even agreed to let him join me on some of my interstate stage spots – it was working! Suzie Q, solo artist, was morphing into one half of a dynamic duo.

There was a downside though. I discovered that my appeal as a Penthouse Pet had dropped significantly. Performing with someone onstage, who you are obviously in love with, kind of breaks the 'single and available' illusion you have when you're alone onstage, making sexually suggestive moves with your naked body. I'd never made so little money off photos and magazine sales before.

I held Toby's face between my hands and quoted a line from Nicole Kidman in *Moulin Rouge!*: 'You're going to be bad for business.'

He gave me a little kiss on the nose, completely unfazed. In fact, he was unfazed by most things – he took photos of me topless with the few adoring male fans who still wanted pictures with me. When they were short an emcee for a sex-toy auction, he grabbed the microphone and a few minutes later was up onstage, waving around a bright pink dildo and shouting numbers at the crowd.

This, I thought to myself, *this is the man for me.*

I took him home to meet my family. They adored him almost as much as I did.

Toby invited me home to rural Wisconsin to meet his. By some miracle, I had a two-week gap in my schedule.

But I hesitated. This was a big step. I called my dad.

'You're a long time dead, Em,' was all he had to say.

I booked my ticket and flew for forty hours to the middle of the American Corn Belt. It was like nothing I'd ever seen before. Fields of rippling green-and-yellow corn stalks as far as I could see. Red barns with white trim and dairy cows with glossy black-and-white coats. It was beautiful.

It was a disaster.

Toby's family had found out my name via his Facebook page and Googled me before I arrived. They were unsure how to treat 'Suzie Q' – a former Miss Nude Australia and Penthouse Pet was something quite outside of their frame of reference.

I was nervous as hell and it was awkward and uncomfortable. I was overwhelmed by the cultural differences. I was used to naked girls, champagne and cash. Not cows, corn, tractor pulls and lawnmower races. I was horrified at the 'pig catch'. I'll never forget the expression on that little Crisco-covered piglet's face when he spotted dozens of excited five-year-olds thundering towards him across the dusty ground. I felt like I couldn't relate to 'these people' and withdrew even further into myself. My introversion did not help me grow any closer to them. I'd copped so much flack over the years from different people that 'being judged' had become part of my identity. Tired of having my work commented on, or being broken up with because of it, meant I already had walls of defence up. I assumed I was being judged, often before I actually had been. It was the same as wearing my pyjamas to school: 'You don't like what I do? Well, we can't be friends then. I'll shut myself off to ensure I can't be hurt by you.'

I had dreamed of having a second 'Mom' to bake pies with (in matching aprons of course!). The dream was shattered. They couldn't understand why their salt-of-the-earth eldest child would want to be with someone 'like that'. And I did nothing to open up, let them in and show them who I was. I felt like they'd already judged Suzie, so why bother showing them Emma?

...

Back home, Toby and I launched into training for the Asia-Pacific Pole Championships. We toyed with the idea of a 'Tarzan and Jane' theme. As we were training different jungle-esque/animalistic movements, people watching asked 'Hey, is that *Avatar?*'

By the time the fifth or sixth person said it, we looked at each other and slowly said 'Ye-es …' at the same time.

Now to figure out how to make ourselves blue.

We eventually settled on blue hairspray – I did a few trials in pole class (teaching with one blue leg) to make sure we'd be safe. There was a lot riding on our winning the Asia Pacifics. An international title was almost essential if Toby was going to join me on a three-month teaching tour around the world next year. We had to be good. Again, I felt like it was my name and reputation on the line. I was 'Suzie Q', wasn't I? And that name meant something, didn't it?

My perfectionism put an incredible amount of strain on our relationship. It couldn't just be good. It had to be *perfect*. I would make Toby do things over and over and over. He practically had to live his life as an Avatar. I even made him vacuum the house and do the washing-up in character.

Toby did his best but couldn't catch onto things as quickly as I would have liked. I wished I had chosen another pole dancer to be my competition partner. Performing with him was fine, but the extra pressure of competing made me snappy and angry.

'Do it AGAIN,' I yelled. 'We don't practice until we get it right. We practice until we can't get it wrong.'

He began to feel like a source of stress to me, rather than the soothing source of peace he had once been.

The night of the competition, I was a nervous wreck. I competed in the Women's Solo Division. (Placing second. Again.) I felt a small snapping sensation in my shoulder during my solo show, but pushed it aside. We pulled off our doubles *Avatar* routine pretty much as planned. Standing onstage during the winners' announcements, I had all my fingers and toes crossed. I mentally repeated, *Please let us win. Please let us win.* We had devoted every spare second to training, going into the studio at 10 p.m. each night once classes were finished, getting home after 12 a.m. We had fought and argued and …

'Suzie Q and Toby J,' boomed the announcer.

I screamed and jumped straight into Toby's arms. He beamed back at me. We had done it! All that hard work and sacrifice had paid off – we had won!

We headed to South Africa the very next week to take a three-week safari before joining the crew at Sexpo in Johannesburg. Three weeks off aerials and pole were a blessing for my freshly injured shoulder. The snap I'd felt during my solo performance was my right rotator cuff tearing. Under strict instructions from my physio, I slung my elastic TheraBand around the front seat of the four-wheel drive, the tent poles, even a tree in the Okavango Delta, to keep up with my rehabilitation exercises as we toured through Africa, before heading into four straight days of pole and trapeze shows. My shoulder held up thanks to 'adrenaline and love' but it was never really the same again.

Life with Toby was frenetic. We made the finals of *Australia's Got Talent* two years in a row. We bought and renovated three properties, as well as putting a new kitchen and paint into my first apartment. He helped build the second Suzie Q Pole Studio when we moved to larger premises in 2009, then helped to design and build another studio when Charlee and I decided to expand interstate. Together, Toby and I travelled all over the world performing, either to perform or judge pole dancing competitions. We did pole shows at high-brow corporate gigs for big companies. Unlike Ashleigh and I, we were never asked to leave. As a male–female team, we offered 'equal opportunity offensiveness'.

We performed at celebrity birthday parties, Cirque du Soleil's Christmas party and were regularly booked to perform at people's weddings. I'd gone from being the Buck's Night entertainment to being the highlight of the wedding reception. We were always so busy; it was stressful. Just like when I'd told Gayna that I'd take a day off when I was sick or injured, I told myself I'd relax and let go when everything on my 'to-do' list was complete.

Of course, this was impossible. I owned my own business and several properties. I managed our performance schedules and tour bookings. It was utterly impossible to ever complete my 'to-do' list. There was always something else that 'urgently' needed my attention. So I kept going, refusing days off or down time, and piling on job after job after job.

Due to some unfortunate scheduling, Miss Pole Dance Australia was held during the middle of the Sexpo. I raced from hosting the amateur strip at Sexpo to competing in Miss Pole (I didn't place) back to Sexpo to do a final trapeze show. It was too much. Too much adrenaline. Too much stress.

The next morning at the show, I collapsed backstage. It was the most intense migraine I have ever experienced. I vomited all day and into the night. Dry-heaving up my stomach lining before Toby took me to the hospital at 2 a.m. They put four bags of fluid in to rehydrate me and, eventually, the dry-retching stopped. Toby stayed the night in hospital with me. Every time I opened my eyes, he was still there. Sitting on a chair in the corner, just watching over me. He took me home in the morning and, for some insane reason, I agreed to do my trapeze shows that afternoon at Sexpo. After being in hospital all night, a few hours later, I was six metres up in the air, feeling decidedly woozy.

Looking back, I should have been feeling decidedly stupid.

I taped my hospital armband to my dresser mirror with **TWO DAYS OFF** written above it. But I didn't learn. All my value came from *doing*. I always had to be doing something. Preferably working. It wasn't *having* the money; it was *earning* the money.

Besides, earning the money could be pretty fun sometimes.

One night we had just finished our shows for the night, and were settling into some well-earned ice cream at a late-night gelato place, when the phone rang. 'Suzie, we need you to come and do a show … (static) … U2 … (more static) … now.'

Although it was after midnight, I was intrigued. 'I think we'd better go,' I told Toby. 'I think I might get to perform for U2.'

We made our way to a favorite performance space of mine. We were ushered inside and I was briefed on my show. 'The guy who is having the Stag Do is wearing a zebra-print hat, make sure you give him some extra attention.' She clacked off in her high heels.

Toby glared at me. 'Are you sure she said U2 on the phone? … Are you sure it wasn't "Stag Do"?'

I stared back helplessly. *Maybe I had heard wrong?*

Toby took my iPod and playlist to the DJ. I began to get changed. Seconds later, he came running back to me, eyes shining and a massive smile on his face.

'Oh, my God, it's not only Bono … Guns N' Roses are here, too!'

My heart leapt. This was undeniably the most illustrious audience I'd ever had! My show felt amazing and magical. I was floating – and casting as many winning smiles as possible at Bono and the other celebrated audience members (not forgetting, of course, zebra-print hat man).

I sauntered off the stage … straight into the arms of Bono, who congratulated me on my performance. Toby, sensing a 'one time only' opportunity, asked for a photo.

This was Suzie Q v3.0. I had gone from stripper to pole dancer to corporate aerialist/celebrity pole performer. I had to pivot, keep reinventing myself. Keep changing so I could keep working. I was being paid to travel the world with my partner and to perform for celebrities – I was living the dream.

Except, I wasn't.

It was so intense that I barely had time to appreciate each moment or each place.

We'd try to take a few days off when we were in different exotic locales but, often, our schedule just wouldn't allow it – we'd see the airport, the convention center, our hotel and then the airport again. It was hard but I never felt displaced or lost. I had Toby and therefore I had my home with me.

Life was so intense that my yoga classes became even more important as a little 'break' in my hectic days. The asana (poses) felt useful. Focusing on splits and backbends – essential for pole – and the sound of my breath through my nose, drowned out my excessive thoughts. The classes were hard, with lots of handstands and complicated arm balances. I would waste my savasana – telling myself I would 'relax and let go in just a second, right after I think about my day/my next show/some choreography/what I'm doing next week.'

An idea had started to form in the back of my mind. *Perhaps I could do yoga teacher training?* I loved going to yoga

– it was a 'time out' from my insane schedule and, more importantly, a 'time out' from my insanely overactive and anxious mind. The little window of peace it provided was magical – I wanted to gift that same space to other people. The trouble was, a 200-hour teacher-training course (the minimum to be qualified) seemed an unreasonable drain on both my time and money. I tried to find a spare two weeks (the shortest course I could find) but there was always some other, more pressing, gig or event in the way. What on Earth would they be covering that could possibly take two whole weeks? Yoga was just some downward dogs and some hamstring stretches, right? I was way too busy to take that much time away from work. Two weeks off work and performing? Unthinkable.

I had just turned twenty-nine and decided to do a BodyBalance teacher training instead. BodyBalance is a choreographed gym program, a mix of yoga, tai chi and Pilates. The training only took one weekend. Not only would I be qualified to teach BodyBalance, I was pretty sure that with the skills I would gain from this I would be able to pull off yoga classes as well. Fake it until you make it, right?

I found a training center and, by a bizarre stroke of luck, the teacher training was the same weekend as Miss Nude ACT – and the strip club wanted me to judge and perform a feature show. The stripping gig paid for my flights and accommodation, and almost covered my training fee as well. I performed Friday night and woke up bleary-eyed on the Saturday, wiping off body glitter and the remnants of smeared black eyeliner to appear at the training center fresh-faced, a model of healthy living.

I bumped into a lady in in the car park. She was wearing a shirt with 'BodyBalance' emblazoned across the front.

'Hi there, are you here for the training?' I asked.

'I'm running the training,' she smiled back at me. She was about fifty, short and slightly overweight with brown hair set in waves close to her head.

'Ah, so I'm Emma on your list – but if you could please call me Suzie.'

She looked bemused rather than confused. 'Your name is Suzie?'

'No, my real name is Emma. But I perform under Suzie Q and I also teach under that name.'

She accepted this and made a note next to my name on the class roll.

The weekend flew by in a blur – I loved every second. There was no mention of yogic philosophy, but even just the body movements and the importance given to the ten-minute relaxation at the end of class felt somehow 'right'. I was glowing as I completed the training. This was me. I felt like I had come home.

I secured some classes shortly afterwards at different gyms back home. Here was a very different approach to my 'time for cash' strategy I'd employed up until now. I would rather drive for up to an hour to teach one Balance class – which netted me $50, rather than teaching three pole classes at my own studio, which paid $225. I loved the blissed-out looks on the faces of my Balance students as they practically floated out of the room.

Chapter 10

The Suzie Q Pole Studio on the coast was not doing as well as the one at home so Toby and I moved up there to help manage it. We bought another house together; it was beautiful. Everything I had ever wanted in a home. I had just turned thirty. I was a property 'millionaire', in the sense that I had over $1 million worth of property. But I also had a lot of debt. I had to keep pushing myself, pushing my body, each week just to meet the crippling mass of mortgage repayments. I felt the need to say 'yes' to any and all work, because it was there and I was scared that the next week, it wouldn't be. I had to be completely self-reliant. Not trusting anyone else – least of all the Universe. The fact was, I felt utterly lost. I had no dreams or goals past this point. All I had was 'Property millionaire. Retire at thirty.' Unsure of what to do next, I looked to the past for answers. Three years had passed since our last title and so, even though it had almost broken us last time, Toby and I decided to jump into the pairs pole competition arena once more.

Chapter 11

Suzie v4.0. The Turning Point

I am 30 years old.

I called it the 'Olympic Swimmers Lifestyle'. Toby and I would wake up, eat a high-protein breakfast and do a training session, then do some admin and computer work. Take a break for lunch then train again. Teach classes in the evening then go for a massage when we finished work that night. When our arms were too tired, or our bodies too sore, we took a day off and walked on the beach, watched movies in bed or caught up on the seemingly endless administration and emails that come as part and parcel of running a business.

For all our efforts and those of our incredible team of staff, the coast studio was not doing well. We had failed to research the demographics of the area sufficiently and the business model from my main studio did not translate to the local market. It is a beautiful holiday destination, with endless stretches of white sandy beaches and an overabundance of recreational activities on offer, from theme parks to fitness centers (with the highest per capita rate of 24-hour gyms anywhere in the country). We were lost in a sea of options and were haemorrhaging large amounts of money each month. The three-year lease we had signed gave us no other option but to change the business structure completely. After seeking the advice of friends, we changed all our classes to casuals, rather than eight-week terms, to suit the more relaxed and transient nature of the population. This helped turn things around and we started breaking even at least, if not actually making money. Throughout the restructure, Toby and I kept up our relentless training schedule. We won the Australian Pole Championships with a surf-lifesaving inspired routine and set our sights on representing Australia in the International Pole Championships.

I have always believed that things in life go to whoever wants it the most. If you're willing to make the sacrifices and put in the hard work, then you can have and achieve anything you want. Although Toby is much more laid back in his approach to life, happy doing whatever, I decided that I could want it enough for the both of us. I was single minded in my focus and determination. 'Olympic Swimmers Lifestyle' stepped up a notch. We created new moves and sought private lessons with industry professionals – anything to give us the slightest edge over the competition. Preparing for the International Championship was my whole focus. My militant teaching style had not mellowed in the slightest over the past few years and Toby copped the brunt of it. I was stressed out about the pressure of competing and took it out on him. I felt him pulling further and further away from me, but didn't understand that I was the cause.

We did have a couple of conversations about what it would mean to win.

'I guess more touring ... Teaching more guest workshops overseas, right?'

'I'm not sure I want to be doing that. I'm a bit over the hectic travel schedule.'

'Yeah. Me too.'

We stared at each other for a moment.

'Oh well, we're this far in now – let's get back to training.'

'Keep on, keeping on' was our way of being together. Work. Training. Meals – these were the glue holding our fragile relationship together.

We flew to Singapore for the Championships. Stayed in the same hotel with all the other pole competitors from around the world – men, women, pairs and even disabled artists – who have devoted their life to pole. You have a special relationship with the other touring pole dancers – only they can truly understand you and your lifestyle, because they live it, too. We caught up with these people – one week in Sydney, the next in Chicago, a year later at a different event in Asia. And now we all converged upon Singapore for the International Pole Championships. It was so much fun hanging out with everyone – if there wasn't that pesky competition hanging over us, it would have been an awesome holiday.

During our tech run, I caught Toby from a drop and then flipped him out of my arms in a backflip. A move we had executed hundreds of times during training.

Only this time, my left knee gave out and I crashed to floor. No pain, it just … stopped working. I stood up and it instantly collapsed out from under me again. I stared at my leg in complete bewilderment. *What the hell was going on?* It didn't hurt. I just couldn't put any weight on it.

I headed backstage to prepare for the show but my knee felt unstable. Like it could give out again at any moment. I didn't trust it. An hour before the curtain went up, the physio for the comp gave me the all-clear and taped it for the show.

I went through my warm-up routine on autopilot. I felt sick. My leg wasn't right. We had spent the better part of the last year preparing for this night. All that work.

'Don't practice until you get it right, practice until you can't get it wrong' saw me through. I could have done that routine in my sleep. And I ended up doing it without a functioning left leg. Those few precious moments when we were together in the air, without any weight on it, it was almost like normal. But as soon as I tried to walk or dance between poles, it awkwardly splayed out to the side. It was like my leg had been replaced with piece of cooked spaghetti. The routine finished, I limped to the side of the stage and collapsed, pale and shaky. I cried.

I cried for all those hours spent in training.

I cried because we had given up friends' birthdays, weddings and fun times together so we could spend our time on a pole. I cried because I had let myself down. I cried because I had let Toby down and the preparation for this comp had felt like the only thing holding us together these past few months. And I cried because I couldn't actually stand up or walk.

It turned out I had a full thickness tear of a ligament on the inside of my knee. I spent the next two days alone in the hotel room rotating ice packs (twenty minutes on, twenty minutes off), struggling down the hallway on crutches to the ice machine, while Toby went out sightseeing with the rest of the pole crew. I felt alone and utterly defeated. I had wanted to win so badly. I had done all the work, put in all the hours, made all the necessary sacrifices. But somehow, it hadn't been enough. I posted pictures on social media, joking that too many people had told me to 'break a leg' but inside, I was wrecked. Even more so when I found out I would need a knee reconstruction if I ever wanted to perform again.

And I did want to perform again. I was a performer. An entertainer. That's me. That's who I am. I viewed the reconstruction as just a small glitch in my hitherto dazzling career. How you do anything is how you do everything. I approached my operation with my usual single-minded determination and 110% of my effort and energy. I researched and interviewed surgeons. For several weeks, I dedicated myself to a 'pre-hab' program of cycling and strengthening exercises. The day after the operation, I busted out a handstand. Just to show myself that I could. Also probably because Toby told me not to.

I spent the first part of my recovery exercising any way I could. I Googled 'workouts for paraplegics' and tried out anything and everything, from using little dumbbells to full ninety-minute 'Chair Yoga' sessions. I really did want to teach yoga. On the bright side, the recovery from the operation meant I suddenly had the time to do that Yoga Teacher Training I'd been putting off for so long. I considered courses in Thailand, Melbourne and the USA, before choosing to attend the Byron Yoga Center Teacher Training. Not because the course came highly recommended (although it did), but mostly because it was the closest, quickest and the course dates fitted in best with my schedule.

I filled in the application form, writing 'Emma' under 'Name' but pausing at 'preferred name'. I always, always wrote 'Suzie' under preferred name. But for some reason, this time I did not. This was something I wanted to do as Emma.

A 200-hour Yoga Teacher Training is life changing. I, and the other teacher trainees on my course, became a tight-knit support group for each other as we each faced our own inner demons and challenges. For the less gregarious trainees, these came in the form of public speaking and leading a class. I smiled sympathetically and doled out hugs to those who were reduced to tears the first time they had to teach in front of the general public. I still loved being 'onstage' and 'on show' and saw teaching as simply an extension of that – with the added bonus that, rather than just offering entertainment, I was providing a bridge between where the students were and where they wanted to be – physically, with pole. And now mentally as well, with yoga.

My own inner struggles came about during meditation component of the course. It turned out that 'yoga' was about 1% the physical poses you did on your mat. Yoga was really about your state of mind when you were off your mat. Due to my lifestyle and insatiable need to be busy all the time, my state of mind off my mat was not what you would call 'calm'. The physical aspect of yoga was easy for my well-trained body. But for my poorly trained mind, meditation felt stupid and impossible. I didn't get it at all. I could sometimes focus on my breath rather than my thoughts for a few seconds, but I'd soon be lost again in the 'thought ball', which was how I referred to the giant, endlessly spinning cloud mass of anxious thoughts in my head. The technical term for this is the 'monkey mind': the idea that our mind is filled with these crazy-ass monkeys, screeching, chattering, jumping around and clamouring for our attention.

Really though, I don't think that term is anymore technical than 'thought ball'.

As part of our assessment, we had to demonstrate we had established a daily meditation practice – keeping a journal of how long we had 'sat' for each day. I tried every trick I could think of to get my mind to settle for these sessions – I would set the timer for only one minute, then two minutes, then back to one. I would spend that minute trying to choose which 'technique' to use: *Breath awareness? Which kind? Ooh – perhaps a mantra meditation? No, I'm just going to feel sensations in my feet for the whole minute. No, no, I'm going to count my breath.* Before I knew it, the time was up and I hadn't even settled on a technique to use. I'd spent thousands of hours training my body, but had never really put any time into training my mind. And it showed. Sure, I read books and listened to educational podcasts, but this was a different kind of training. And my mind felt really, really unfit.

I wasn't sure what I was doing, but was pretty sure it wasn't meditating. Mostly, I sat and made lists of all the things I had to do that day. Sometimes I would set the timer for ten minutes and stop after five, because the need to check my emails was too strong. Richard's words from a time long-past in a five-star hotel came back to me. I mentally whispered, *Mind over mind. Mind over mind,* over and over to myself. Well, sort of. It would actually be about three or four times before I was distracted by something else. No matter what technique I chose to try and soothe it, my mind still whirled. It felt like the practice was getting harder, not easier, over time. I tried guided meditations, breath awareness, body scans, sitting on the floor, sitting on a chair, lying down, eyes closed, eyes open, being outside, being inside and mantra meditations, whereby you repeat a key word or phrase over and over to hold your mind's attention. I found *I am present* to be the most ironic of these, because I rarely was. It was a miracle if I could get to ten minutes without checking my phone partway through – not just checking how much time was left, but literally checking my phone for messages, emails or Facebook. All these things that were seemingly much more 'important' at the time. I would try and do anything rather than sit and just be.

Towards the end of the course, we were told to sit and meditate for twenty minutes. I freaked out. I sat and cried quietly for the entire time – no sympathetic smiles or warm hugs from my classmates to comfort me. Even though I was surrounded by people, I was utterly alone with my mind and thoughts. I snuck a look out of half-closed eyes only to see everyone looking completely serene and still, sitting like perfect little Buddha statutes – completely unaware of the tumultuous battle going on inside my mind and against myself. Rather than *Mind over mind*, this was *Mind versus mind*, and there could be no winner. I just kept repeating to myself, *I can't do this. This is too hard for me. I can't do it*, as tears softly rolled down my cheeks. We had been told to count our breath up to 100.

Breathing in – *One.*

Breathing out – *Two.*

Breathing in – *Three.*

Breathing out – *Four.*

But I could barely manage:

Breathing in – *One.*

Breathing out …

Before descending back into the hell I was creating for myself with my thoughts.

Breathing in –

I can't.

Breathing out –

Do this.

Breathing in –

I can't.

Breathing out –

Do this.

Every second was agony. My back hurt, one of my feet had gone to sleep and I felt utterly broken. I wanted to get up and run screaming from the room – but didn't want to disturb the other people in my class. It was the longest twenty minutes of my life. It felt impossible. They say that the yoga pose you hate the most is the one you need the most. This endless impossible agony was something I 'needed'? *Bullshit. No one needs this torture.*

And then, suddenly, out of the extreme silence, a bell sounded. It was over. I opened my eyes and lifted my head as the clear sound reverberated around the room. Relief and rational thought flooded through my body. *I had made it!* Now that it was over and I could look back from the perspective of no longer being in it, I wondered if perhaps it had really been so bad after all? I realised the main reason it felt so bad was because I had sat there telling myself how awful and how hard it was.

Instantly, I saw how I had made other, seemingly idyllic situations in my life into my own personal hell through the power of my thoughts. I was experiencing a strange mix of emotions simultaneously – a sombre state of reflection, mixed with light-filled elation that I had made it. Sure I hadn't 'meditated' at all (whatever that was). But who cared? I had sat (relatively) still for twenty minutes. That which had seemed beyond impossible had actually been achieved. My joy was tempered with concern at the wider and broader implications of this new-found knowledge about my mind. Had Toby's family really been judgemental? Was Toby really 'too laid back' for me? Or was that just a story my mind had made up? Was running a business really all that stressful? Or was that a story, too?

I sipped chai with the other graduates. We hugged and said our goodbyes. I felt close to them – extraordinarily close, considering we'd known each other for less than two weeks. I think perhaps because the Suzie Switch was in the 'off' position (mostly) I'd actually let people in. These were the first people I had let use 'the E-word' in more than ten years. They had got to know Emma and, not only that – they had actually liked her.

It can be difficult to acclimatise to real life once you leave the 'yoga bubble'. I was very lucky that, as soon as I left my first teacher training at the Byron Yoga Center, I flew straight to Ohio for another teacher training. This time it was in Rocket Yoga – hard yoga. Power yoga. Lots of handstands and arm balances. Less sitting around doing 'nothing'. Much more my style. My teacher thought it was hilarious that, while most women come to Ashtanga or Rocket Yoga to become stronger, I had in fact come to it to be softer. I thought it was hilarious that I'd come here to train 'yoga' when the word itself means 'comfortable seat'. The whole reason you do yoga poses is so you can sit comfortably in seated meditation for long periods of time.

Damn it.

And so my daily struggles with meditation continued. There was little-to-no respite from my relentless thinking. Except when I was training handstands with my instructor – I couldn't think about much else when I was balancing on my hands. Perhaps this is also why I love performing so much. There is that same sense of single-minded focus. I asked her if I couldn't possibly just do 'performing meditation'? She laughed. She told me that one day my strengths would become my weakness and my weaknesses would become my strengths.

I assumed she was referring to my knee reconstruction; sometimes, I felt frustrated at how long it was taking to recover its former ability. But mostly, I just felt grateful that every day it was a little better than the day before.

'Plus,' I told my teacher, 'I'm going to be so good at teaching yoga to people with knee injuries.'

They say that the recovery time for any injury is dependent, firstly, on how bad you think the injury is and, secondly, on why you think you incurred the injury. I was convinced the reason I'd injured my knee was simply to allow me to complete my yoga teacher training. And so, when I returned home, a mere three months after my surgery, Toby and I were back performing. We modified our shows – so my new knee was not at risk and I promised myself I would take it easier this time – not pack my schedule so tightly and, instead, leave space to just stop and chill out occasionally.

Maybe I would even start taking those two days off each week.

But the lure of work called me with its siren song. Two days off was quickly reduced to one, then none. Suzie Q Pole Studio was asked to present at a fitness expo so I prepared a speech and choreographed shows for my staff and me. It was a big week – rehearsals during the day then teaching until late each night. Falling into bed, exhausted but tossing and turning, struggling with the thought ball, until the small hours before dropping off to sleep.

Chapter 11

All that meditation and yoga training had not helped my insomnia. I still wasn't able to sleep, but at least now I felt more relaxed about it.

After a big week of overtraining and not really sleeping, I took to the stage at Slide with Toby and, towards the end of our routine, whatever tiny thread had been holding my shoulder together for the last few years finally snapped. Thankfully, we were one trick away from the end of the routine. I finished, bowed and made my way to the change room. My arm hung limply by my side. I felt sick. I knew it was bad. I couldn't even lift our costume bag into the car. We drove home with makeshift ice packs (ice wrapped in napkins) tightly packed all around me.

With great disappointment, I was going back on my word and letting the team down, I pulled out of the fitness expo. I cancelled the rest of my shows for that weekend and stayed in bed. Twenty minutes on and twenty minutes off with ice packs again, for the next two days.

I think I knew, deep down, that I'd just pushed too hard, too far, for too long. Something was bound to give, eventually.

And something just had.

I was booked on a yoga retreat three days later. I did as much as I could, holding my arm up like a crippled paw whenever we were on all fours, and more than a little disappointed that I couldn't show off my handstand skills. One night there was a Kirtan – kind of like a yogic dance party. Dancing around with wild and reckless abandon (not too reckless though, in case somebody banged into my arm), I felt more joy than I'd felt in a long time. I wasn't dancing because a man was paying me to, or because I was trying to teach a woman to move in a 'sexy' way. I was free. Free and perfect. This way of moving, this way of being – surrounded by people who radiated joy out of every pore – was so different to the life I had known. Nobody was pretending. It made me start to question everything I had known. When I was honest, 'everything I had known' wasn't really working for me anymore. I was tired. I was burnt-out and my body was wrecked. I felt, as J.R.R. Tolkien so beautifully described it, 'Thin … Like butter that has been scraped over too much bread.' But I had no idea what to do about it.

It was like nothing was working. I needed to change everything. Changing everything seemed scary. Actually, it seemed stupid. But in an instant I knew, with absolute certainty, everything was about to change.

...

Back in reality after the spell cast by the Kirtan, I tried every kind of therapy available – physio, osteo, chiro, essential oils, massage, cortisone injections – even injections of bovine cartilage – anything to avoid going back under the surgeon's knife.

Those same questions about my identity flooded through me once more. I was a pole dancer and aerialist. I had just returned to my career from my knee surgery. If I had to have shoulder surgery, I could no longer do those things. I would no longer *be* those things. Possibly ever again.

Chapter 11

Who was I?

It was too much. I needed to get away, take a break. So Toby and I took a holiday in Bali to give my shoulder a rest. It was our first-ever time travelling without working. Except that I spotted a sign in a café in Ubud: 'Yoga Teacher Needed Urgently.'

Without telling Toby, I called the number.

'Hi. This is Suzie. I saw your ad. I'd like to come and teach for you.'

'Can you be here tomorrow?'

I looked over at Toby, who was staring sceptically at his superfood-antioxidant-green smoothie.

'Sure,' I replied.

The next day, we were at the retreat center – me teaching yoga and Toby hanging out with the locals, learning the traditional Indonesian way to make bricks and thatch and carve coconuts. I taught or did yoga twice a day and spent the rest of my time in a hammock, drinking coconuts and reading *The Power of Now*

Reading Eckhart Tolle's words, I began to feel a bit sick. How much of my life had I actually missed? I had been in some amazing places and had some amazing experiences. But for how many of them had I actually been present? I was always rushing to the next thing. Planning our next act, doing choreography in my head or replying to emails. How many friends and family birthdays, weddings, anniversaries and life events had I missed because I was working? I had all these weird and wonderful opportunities and experiences, but how many of them did I fully experience when I was always wishing and planning that I was somewhere else? My suicide attempt and subsequent recovery meant I was technically on 'bonus time' and here I was, wasting it and ruining it, choosing to be consumed by my thoughts, not enjoying every precious extra minute I had been granted. Whatever was occupying my mind always seemed more important than being present to whatever was actually happening in the moment.

The only time I was truly present was when I was onstage. And even then, when things went wrong in our acts (which they invariably did) I'd get so angry at myself, at Toby, at the world. Perfection was everything. Having a knee reconstruction forced me to slow down enough to reflect on my life and gave me time to complete my yoga teacher training. However, it seemed like I'd missed whatever the Universe was trying to communicate to me. Having exhausted all other options, my shoulder reconstruction was scheduled for June 2015.

We had one final aerial performance booked. Contracts had already been signed. I'd given my word and I didn't want to let anyone down so agreed to go through with the performance. If I said I was going to be somewhere, or if I was going to do something, then I damn-well did it. Regardless of the cost to myself. Sometimes the relentless ambition of Suzie Q, who didn't let anyone else down, actually let Emma down.

'What the hell do you think you're doing?' asked my dad, when he found out I intended to perform. 'Your shoulder will SNAP if you go on a trapeze.'

His words echoed in my head for the entire performance.

Chapter 11

It is going to snap, it is going to snap, I kept repeating over and over to myself. I wasn't fully present in my body or my movement, because I was so worried about my shoulder, whether or not it was going to make it through the show. Six metres up is not a good time to lose focus and, sure enough, I accidentally started doing the wrong routine.

'What are you doing?' hissed Toby.

'I've f***ed up, haven't I?' I whispered back. 'It's okay. I'll fix it.'

Toby, the best base ever, just followed along with the new 'routine' I was creating. We finished in time with the music and the crowd was none the wiser. I don't even think they noticed our little chat in the middle of our show.

Worried about how I would earn an income after my operation, I enrolled for a Yin Yoga teacher training – Yin is a gentle form of yoga practice, less about pushing your body to its physical limits and more about releasing and surrendering into each pose. I hoped Yin would 'break me' and rid me of my monkey mind once and for all.

Turns out that in the complete stillness of your physical body, your mental activity is actually highlighted. How you are on your mat is a reflection of how you are off it and my mind was, as always, screamingly busy. What I hadn't realised is that Yin Yoga is uncomfortable. Really uncomfortable. I was desperate to move, adjust, readjust *– I'll be comfortable if only … I move this blanket, move my arm, change the angle of my leg …* I realised this sounded an awful lot like: *I would be happy if only … Toby was as motivated* *as I was; if only … I didn't have a business to run … my staff vacuumed more often … my shoulder wasn't so damaged.*

A guest teacher came in to introduce us to Buddhist philosophy. Mr Buddhism sat stock still for two hours and spoke about 'Right Thought, Right Action and Right Livelihood'. The sex trade was specifically excluded from this last category and I waited for him after class, ready to pounce on the opportunity for an argument and the chance to defend my former profession.

I politely explained that I had been an exotic dancer and asked, 'Why, exactly, is that excluded from being considered a "Right" livelihood?'

'Why were you a dancer?'

I was impressed that he hadn't said stripper.

'Money,' was my succinct reply.

'And do you think that was a truly altruistic motivation?'

I had paid almost $2000 for this course … I wondered how 'altruistic' *his* motivations were for teaching. 'Would *you* show up here if you weren't being paid?'

He ignored my question.

'So why don't you strip now?'

I paused. 'I guess, I'm in a different space now. And making men fall in love with me for money doesn't feel right anymore.'

I hadn't noticed myself changing from the money-hungry sexpot, who was quite happy cavorting naked in front of strangers, to the girl standing in yoga tights with an 'Om' symbol around her neck, arguing about Buddhist philosophy in the hallway of a yoga studio. It made me wonder even more, *Who am I? Clearly, I'm not Suzie Q the stripper, pole dancer or aerialist anymore … What's left?*

Emma?

Was this Emma?

I felt like none of the 'Suzie things' were working anymore. My body had let me down, the studio was more a source of stress than a source of fun and my relationship with Toby – which had always had its own ups and downs – was definitely experiencing a big downward spiral. It felt like I had had a deal with the Universe. The deal was: I achieved what I set out to do; I was a property millionaire and able to retire at thirty. Pushing past that, in any way, wasn't part of the deal. The Universe lets you know when it's time to move on. First it taps you, then it kicks you, then it sends you a shoulder reconstruction.

It was an 'exploratory surgery'. Despite the numerous scans I'd had, they didn't know exactly what was wrong. They were going to open me up, find what was broken and fix it.

It was petrifying walking into the operating theatre. I expected that I would be sedated and wheeled in unconscious like for my knee. Instead it was just my little bare feet padding across the cold floor. I was naked apart from the hospital-issue mesh underwear and gown. My gown only had one arm through – I clutched it around my breasts to try and hide the nudity I was usually so proud to show off. I felt very small. The room was lit all around with bright, bright lights and all manner of surgical instruments. I climbed up onto the bed. Only it wasn't a bed; it was a stainless-steel bench. The surgical team gathered around me, with their hats and masks, I felt remarkably like I was about to be probed on an alien space ship.

'Trapeze artist, eh?' asked the anaesthetist, 'I used to do that.'

I felt the cold sting of the needle in my arm.

'Really? Whereabouts did you …'

I woke up in recovery and looked up at a passing nurse. 'Is it done? Is it over?'

She gestured to my wrapped and padded right side.

Yes. It was done. But I was yet to find out what *it* was. When the surgeon came by, I learned they had stapled down part of my rotator cuff and detached then reattached my biceps tendon further down my arm, securing it in place with a very sweetly named 'biceps button'.

...

Perhaps due to a lack of preparation and pre-hab, my recovery was not as smooth as with my knee. I was depressed. I couldn't exercise and I don't know if you've tried brushing your teeth with your left hand, but it's frustratingly hard. It also takes much longer, which I think is what annoyed me the most. If my knee injury had been for me to do my yoga teacher training, what the hell was this for?

My dad came to visit me. We sat in a café, where I opened up about my life and how unhappy I was.

'Dad, seriously, nothing in my life is working for me anymore.'

'Change it. You're not a tree.'

'Dad, it's everything. It's ALL THE THINGS. The

things I've worked so hard for. Everything is just so ... so ... tangled'

'It took you eight years to knot up this ball of string. It will take some time to undo it.'

'But how do I change everything in my life?'

'You just decide.'

He pulled out a piece of A4 paper and drew a line going from the bottom halfway to the top.

'You're here.' He paused the pen. 'And right now. Today. You're deciding to change direction. You're are deciding to turn left.' He moved the pen towards the left side of the page.

'How?' I asked plaintively.

'Just DECIDE.' He looked at me seriously. 'What's your number-one priority, right now?'

'I don't know. It used to be earning money, but now I'm not ...'

He interrupted me abruptly. 'Your number-one priority is your physical and mental health!'

'So that means I need to change everything? *Everything* in my life?'

'If that's what it takes.'

'But I'm supposed to rearrange the internals not the externals.'

'Perhaps these external changes are a result of the internal changes you're experiencing?'

'When did you get all spiritual and profound?'

'I'm your father. I've always been profound. You just haven't always listened. What's your number-one priority?'

'My mental and physical health' I answered dutifully.

I still kept up my daily 'meditation' practice, if you could call it that. Doggedly sitting for twenty minutes each day. Unsure if I was doing it right. Not even sure if it was doing anything at all.

Despite my dad's words of wisdom, I still didn't know what to do about my life. I sought advice from friends, from family, from psychics. Toby and I had just bought our dream home – a beautiful property on a couple of acres in the Gold Coast hinterland. We'd even bought chickens. I had the life for which I'd been striving for so long. I travelled. I performed. I had a beautiful house and a successful business. Was I seriously proposing to throw all that away? Like it was nothing? People would kill for my life, and here I didn't even want it. I felt ungrateful.

Toby said I bossed him around like a drill sergeant. (He was right.) I felt like he didn't stand up to me or really see me in a romantic way. I probably had overblown expectations, from being treated like a princess by customers in strip clubs for so many years. He was still distant from me and, deep down, I assumed that he must no longer love me. I felt like once people got to know me, really got to know me, there was no way they could possibly love me. From Chris and other boyfriends, to my Dad circling job ads in my kitchen, I always felt like there was something wrong with me. That I wasn't okay as long as I was doing what I did. I didn't want anyone to see whatever was broken inside of me so I spent my entire life trying to hide it. By achieving. By doing. By working. And I had dragged Toby into this vortex with me. Demanding he live up to my impossibly high expectations. Ironically, the result of this was that he felt like he wasn't good enough, that there was something wrong with *him*.

...Although we had spoken about breaking up before, we had always had some big job on the horizon, some cool overseas trip, some contract we'd already signed – something we were working towards. Together. As a team.

However, with my shoulder out of action, I couldn't fulfil any of our obligations. We lived together simply as partners. We were not performing. Not training. Not rehearsing. It suddenly and starkly highlighted the fact that, when we weren't doing those things that kept us so, so busy, we actually had very little in common. Things hit boiling point one night, when he was mucking around with some friends. As he play-wrestled one of the girls to the floor, the look of absolute joy on his face made my decision for me – he hadn't looked that happy in years. I knew being with me was making him miserable. And it was no fun for me, being with someone so distant they were more like a flatmate.

I told him, 'I can't do this anymore,' and ran away to stay with my mom.

I needed my mom.

I threw myself into work at the studio to try and distract myself from the implications of what I'd just done. At least now, I knew why I'd been sent a shoulder reco.

I still sat for twenty minutes each morning. Sometimes just quietly crying to myself. Letting fat tears plop onto my lap. Sometimes Mom would sit with me. The reason I had enrolled in my Yin Teacher Training was the hope that it would break me. Break through my anxiety. Help me to stop trying so damn hard. I kept in touch with Mr Buddhism after the course. He made fun of me, saying that he had never seen anyone who was trying so hard to stop trying so hard.

The Yin teacher training failing to provide the breakthrough I so strongly desired, I enrolled in a Vipassana meditation course. The minimom length of time for your first course was ten days. So here I was, less than twelve months from crying when told to sit and meditate for twenty minutes to willingly subjecting myself to ten hours a day of seated meditation for ten days straight.

Why?

Perhaps to prove to myself that I could.

...

A Vipassana course is known as a 'Retreat' but it's not a feel-good-green-smoothie-hippie-yoga retreat. Vipassana is brutal. Ten days of no phone, no internet, no reading, no writing, no talking, no eye contact, no communication with the outside world and no communication with the other people on the course. No Facebook for ten days. Shit.

Men and women are kept completely separate (to avoid any sexual misconduct). There is no exercise beyond walking, no yoga and, most distressingly of all, no dinner.

You wake each day at 4 a.m. for a 4:30 a.m. two-hour meditation session. You then have breakfast, you sit again, lunch, sit, a break, sit, an evening lecture and you sit again, before heading to bed about 9 p.m. and repeating the whole process again the next day.

The idea is that you feel what is happening in your body and notice your reaction to it. 'Feel sensations. Don't react.' And OMG, the sensations in my hips and back from sitting stock still, cross-legged on a cushion on the floor for that amount of time each day were intense. A blowtorch being fired into my knee, an ice pick lodged in my lower back … About halfway through, I was convinced I'd either have a new set of hips, or desperately need a new set of hips. Three of the daily sessions are known as 'sittings of strong determination'. You do not move for the entire sixty minutes. You don't open your eyes, you don't readjust anything, you don't brush a stray hair from your face. You simply sit. You feel sensations. You don't react. Well, at least you attempt not to move. The first few times we did these, I still found myself shuffling and readjusting throughout.

I kept repeating the parting words of Mr Buddhism: 'It will be challenging, but it will be worth it.' In hindsight, he really should have rephrased this to: 'It will be shit-hard and you will cry and want to leave on day two.' Honestly, if the management had not taken my keys, phone and wallet, I probably would have quietly snuck out.

I was just too stubborn to go and ask for my keys.

On my worst day (Day Three), I found myself wandering aimlessly up and down the bushland track we were allowed to use for exercise during our breaks. I felt like a dog pacing up and down a small fence to which it was tethered unwillingly. I felt like I'd bitten off more than I could chew – this was simply too hard for me. I needed to leave. Tears welled up in my eyes. I had been beaten by Vipassana. No one else was out on the track and so I began to (very softly) sing 'Let It Go' from *Frozen*. It felt like the words had been written for me, at this moment during Vipassana. *It's time to see what I can do, to test the limits and break through.*

I was definitely at my limit. However halfway through the second chorus, a sense of calm determination began to settle over me, I began to wonder if this was just like my first twenty-minute meditation session. *What if it isn't actually as bad as I think it is? What if, maybe, I can actually do this? What if I'm stronger than I think I am?*

I made an appointment to see the teacher.

I was ushered into her private quarters, where I reverently knelt in front of her. I raised my eyes to meet hers and spoke completely honestly, from my heart.

'This is shit.'

She stared at me, bemused.

'Seriously, I don't want to be here.'

'Emma,' she said calmly. It felt weird having my name spoken out loud. 'No one wants to be here. Who in their right mind would subject themselves to this?'

I stared at her, open mouthed and uncomprehending. I'd been expecting some kind of motivating spiritual-speak. About aligning my chakras with the power of the Universe or something. I wasn't sure what to say to brutal honesty. I decided to respond with brutal honesty.

'I'm not taking it seriously. I don't think I'm meditating. I'm not even sitting still.'

'That's why they're called sittings of 'strong determination'. You have to make a strong determination. Maybe move only every second time you want to. Then every third time. You just have to decide.'

Just decide. She sounded like my dad.

Suddenly, it hit me. *This* was the power of 'mind over mind' Richard mentioned all those years ago. I just had to *decide*. In each moment, it was up to me to *decide*.

I went into the next sitting of 'strong determination' with a newfound sense of motivation. I sat. My back hurt. I chose not to move. My face felt itchy. I chose not to scratch. My body felt crooked, like I needed to readjust. I didn't. This continued on and on for an interminably long period of time. Finally, I couldn't take it any longer. I collapsed forward, feeling relief flood through my aching back, just as the bell went signifying the end of the session. *ARGH!!!* I screamed in my head. *So close! Only a couple of seconds longer and I would have made it.* But I wasn't disappointed. I was so, so proud of myself. I had felt my sensations and made a deliberate choice not to buy into them. I was beaming as I exited the meditation hall. I had gone from bawling for twenty minutes to holding completely still for 59:50! #winning! This is not to say it got easier. Many of those 4:30 a.m. meditation sessions I spent craning my eyeballs, trying make out the tiny hands on the watch of the guy across from me in the men's section. Desperate to find out when the torture would end.

I fantasised about Mr Buddhism. I fantasised about leaving the pole studio. About leaving pole dancing altogether. Whenever my eyes snapped open (which was often, even during some of the 'sittings of strong determination'), I would see my name-tag in front of me on the floor. '**Emma Corbett**' spelled out in black bold letters.

Who even is that? I wondered to myself.

It was like trying to connect to someone who doesn't exist. And in a sense, she didn't – you couldn't Google her, she didn't have a Facebook page. How do you find yourself when you've spent seventeen years living as someone else? I don't mean to sound schizophrenic, but am I two people? Am I just one? Suzie is still me, but she is those distilled elements of me that spun out of the centrifuge all those years ago.

I fought so hard to be Suzie. To be accepted as a stripper. To be accepted as a pole dancer. By my parents; by society as a whole. I get to teach pole dancing, to travel, I could pole dance all day if I wanted to. But I don't want to. It doesn't make my heart sing. And, in that, I am doing a disservice to my students. As a teacher, I can inspire others with my passion. If that passion isn't there, I'm not inspiring anyone. Least of all myself.

I would snap back out of these moments of reverie and try again. There were a few moments of meditation. Of stillness. I was aware of very subtle sensations in my body: a sense of tingling, of buzzing. My body felt so very *alive*. Perhaps I was finally feeling the energies that Richard had first mentioned to me, when he twiddled that fork into a spiral under the table? I began to understand where I was trying to go every time I sat to meditate. A space of non-existence. Of nothingness. I could only touch it for a few moments at a time, but it meant I was excited to get into the hall for the next session.

Of course, in the next session I would feel nothing. Couldn't get there at all. Ah yes, that gap between reality and expectations. I got it. Sometimes it would be magical. Sometimes it wouldn't. The key was not to have expectations about how it would go.

On Day Seven, I started to feel an unpleasant pull around the graft in my knee. I made another appointment to see the teacher. I explained my recent surgeries and, thankfully, was moved off my cushion on the floor into a chair.

A chair! Nothing had ever felt so good. I made a 'strong determination' not to move through the next session and actually made it. What's more – I made it with barely an ache or a pain in my body. Sitting in the chair, I was almost comfortable.

Oh no, I had a sudden thought. *How am I going to do this without the sensation of pain to focus on?*

The Universe has a sick sense of humor sometimes because, after the next time I went to the bathroom, I noticed my backside didn't quite feel right. I continued through the rest of the day's sittings but, when I woke up the next morning, I was in agony. Through tears and gritted teeth, I made yet another appointment to see the teacher. I knelt in front of her again and blurted out:

'I think there's something wrong with my butt.'

'What?'

'My butt. I think I've had like an anal prolapse or something.'

'Are you serious?'

I just looked at her with a pained expression on my face, faint traces of tears in my eyes.

'I'm a nurse, well, a paediatric nurse, but I could look at it?'

'Would that be weird?'

'Yeah, that would be weird, wouldn't it?'

'Well, I mean, I don't think it's weird. I just don't want *you* to think it's weird.' I was thinking about all the people who had already seen my ass. Possibly half of Sydney. One more person really didn't worry me.

'It's okay with me. I'll be at your room in half an hour.' She paused. 'I might see if I can find some latex gloves.'

I gave a little bow (I wasn't sure what else to do) and carefully made my way out of the interview room.

I vacuumed, swept and scrubbed my room. I made the bed and closed the curtain.

I took my pants off and lay on my side in the foetal position.

This could only happen to me, I thought, as she prodded around my rear end.

'It's a haemorrhoid,' she declared.

'Really?'

'Yup. A pretty big one.'

'But I haven't prolapsed?'

'No' she laughed. 'I'll get some cream sent in for you and maybe some Panadol. Sitting on that is going to be very uncomfortable.'

I raised my eyebrows at her. 'Thank God I don't have to do much sitting here.'

She gave me a wry smile and left.

I'd been worried that I wouldn't be in enough pain after being moved from the cushion to the chair, but it seemed the Universe had delivered.

Thanks Universe. Big thumbs-up to you.

I believe I am the only person ever to have been anally fingered on a Vipassana Retreat.

If I had been miserable before, now I was utterly despondent. In between sits, I lay on the cold bathroom floor (and gave quiet thanks I had a private ensuite) with my legs up around my ears, a mirror in one hand and the cream applicator in the other.

I couldn't help but think that this, perhaps, was not my finest hour.

The meditation sessions seemed even longer than before. I folded my scarf into a little donut shape and tried to place it surreptitiously under my backside before settling into my chair.

This thing is ruining my Vipassana experience, I thought. I sounded like a whinging little kid: 'It's wrecking iiiiiit.' I realised I was doing what I always did. Arguing with reality. This never ended well for me. Reality always kicked my ass. I began to realise that Frank (I'd given it a name) was not ruining my Vipassana experience. It was part of my Vipassana experience. Once I settled into accepting this, I began to have a much better time. It was a relief to not have my phone constantly pinging and to have nowhere I needed to be (except in the meditation hall). It was a nice reminder that I was a human being, not a human doing.

Driving out of the center at the end of my ten days, I cranked my new theme song, 'Let it Go', as loud as my car speakers could handle. I hung my head out the window, singing, 'It's time to see what I can do / To test the limits and break through' at the top of my lungs as I rocketed down the freeway.

Chapter 12

Becoming Emma.

I am 33 years old.

Letting go is exactly what I did.

I let go of all the 'things' that I'd sacrificed so much to achieve, all the 'things' that I'd thought made me, me.

I had already broken up with Toby. I was still reeling from that decision when Charlee rang me to make plans for the next PoleCandy, our merchandise line and the two studios… My enthusiasm for all things Suzie Q was at an all-time low.

'Can I please come and see you. I have to talk to you.'

'Can't you just say it now?'

'I think it needs to be said face-to-face.'

We'd been through so much together. I'd been there through her divorce, her new house, two of her kids finishing school. She'd been there through the whole romance and break-up with Toby, me moving interstate, all my travels. Charlee had been the one constant in my life for almost eight years.

My voice was hoarse and I couldn't say the words. She said them for me.

Emma Lea Corbett

'You're leaving the studio, aren't you?'

I nodded into the phone as the tears began to fall.

'Yes,' I finally croaked out.

She switched into business mode almost immediately, organising the closure of the coast studio (our three-year lease was finally up) and the necessary paperwork.

I felt like I was walking through a battlefield, with huge bombs going off all around me. Explosions of dust and fire engulfing everything around me and great clouds of smoke billowing up into the sky, as I firebombed all there was in my life in the space of six months. Rather than staying and feeling uncomfortable, I Ganeshed that shit.

I Ganeshed the shit out of it.

My mind kept screaming, *WHAT THE FUCK ARE YOU DOING?? GO BACK. GO BACK!* I wanted to undo it, apologise, press Delete, Backspace, Control+Z. Anything!

But I didn't.

Emma was emerging, pulling me forward, and Suzie Q was kicking and screaming and trying to claw her way back to the life she had always known. I was lucky, in a way, that they had different names and different personalities. It made it easier to distinguish between the two, although it did make me feel a little schizophrenic. I knew I had needed Suzie to protect me, when I was a teenager working in strip clubs. Her strength was what helped me survive the seamy underworld that otherwise could have pulled me under. But beneath that tough-as-nails hard shell, lay a gooey marshmallow center that I was trying to protect. I had viewed that vulnerability and softness as weakness and, perhaps, as a teenager in a strip club, it would have been. But now, that which I had seen as weakness was actually strength. I was reconnecting with the soul that lay beneath the role; it was my vulnerability that made me strong, because that was what made me human.

Don't get me wrong. I used to *love* what I did. I didn't want to take holidays or time off, because I had a life I didn't need a holiday from. The journey had been crazy and insane and fun, but it wasn't fun anymore. I kept clinging to it, hoping it would be fun again. But it wasn't.

And so I set about annihilating all the trappings of Suzie Q.

Toby and I sold the Dream House. It was beautiful; it was everything I had ever wanted. It represented the culmination of years of hard work and focused effort. But, actually owning it, having the chickens, the co-ordinated kitchenware and tea towels, didn't bring me the sense of joy and happiness I'd thought it would. To be honest, it was an expensive Band-Aid for Toby's and my ailing relationship.

We began to inform clients that we were no longer performing together. The phone would ring: 'Would you and Toby like to come and perform on a cruise ship?'

Hell yes we would!

'No. I'm sorry. Toby and I are no longer working together.'

I did try performing with different partners. But it wasn't the same. I think that, by the end, what I truly loved about performing was that I got to share it with

Toby. And now that was gone, too. I was standing on shifting sands. Nothing was stable beneath me anymore.

...

One of the sayings used in Mindfulness teachings is: 'Isn't that interesting'. Like you're looking in at your life from the outside. From an outsider's perspective, I guess my crumbling sandcastle would have been a fascinating study into what constitutes identity. Take someone apart completely – remove their home, relationship, career, business, peer groups and pets (our poor chickens got eaten by a fox) – and see what's left.

When the dust finally settled, I assumed what would be left would be Emma, because she had been missing in action for over a decade, covered over by all this 'Suzie stuff'. I'd barrelled the whole way through my twenties, single-minded in my determination to be a property millionaire and retire by thirty. I was so focused on my goal, I gave absolutely no thought to what this 'retirement' would feel or look like. I just knew I would be happy then, I would relax then, I would let go and enjoy then.

Except, when I achieved it, I just felt … lost.

And more than a little stupid for not thinking of this before.

I was so good at setting goals, how could I have not set any for after age thirty?

That equation I wrote out when I was 17?

House + Loving Relationship + Satisfying Career = ☺

It's wrong.

I should have just written:

Be happy now

When Toby and I started looking at splitting up all our assets, that was when the true futility of my life fully hit me. I had given everything to buy these properties. I had sold views of the inside of my vagina to pay for them, and now half of them were gone? What was the freaking point of the last ten years? It was sickening to realise that all the things I fought for, stressed over, lost countless nights of sleep over – didn't actually matter. Clinging so hard to properties, my career, Toby and the name 'Suzie Q'.

I had thought that what I did was so important. That I was so important. It was startling and very, very humbling to realise the world continued to turn without me doing so much. Without me doing anything, actually. The juggernaut that is Suzie Q Pole Studio rolls on just fine without me.

...

So now I am starting over.

Like a phoenix rising? More like that first time in six-inch heels; like a baby gazelle struggling to stand up for the first time. Stumbling and unsure. Crashing into everything. I keep reassuring myself that, at least at the end of this, I will be a really good Mindfulness teacher. I can legitimately stand in front of people and say, 'In my honest experience, fame, money, a loving partner and a nice house do not guarantee happiness.'

Or as one of my teachers put it, 'Success is not about what you get. It's about what you can give up.'

Suzie Q points her finger at him and yells, 'You'd fucking better be right, buddy!'

231

But I do get what he means.

Once I accepted that even without all the glitz and glamour of 'Suzie Life', without all the things I thought were 'who I am', I still had everything I needed, I began to feel the same sense of liberation that I had experienced after my suicide attempt. I had no house, no job, no pets, no relationship and no career. No commitments.

Real freedom.

The whole world was open to me. I could do anything. Go anywhere. Be anyone.

I decided to be Emma.

I had no idea who that was, but that was okay – neither did anyone else. She only existed as a set of infinite possibilities. My identity was shifting again, only this time I was not reinventing, not creating; I was going back to what was already inside of me.

For the first time in my life, though, I wasn't really sure what I was doing. There was no comp to prepare for, no house that needed renovating, I didn't need to update the social media pages for the pole school or organise staff rosters and payroll. The empty pages of my diary made me nervous. There was empty space there and space needed to be filled. Didn't it?

I called Ashleigh, who by now was married with two kids. 'I just don't know what I'm doing with my life,' I wailed to her.

'Well, you've just completed three different yoga teacher trainings over the past twelve months. Do you think, perhaps, that's a clue?'

She had a point. I loved the changes that yoga and

meditation had brought into my life. I was less stressed, less reactive. I'd even started incorporating Buddhist philosophy into the pole workshops I still taught occasionally. 'It's about the journey, not the destination, girls! Enjoy and explore each part of the movement, don't be in such a hurry to get to the end result and POINT YOUR FUCKING TOES!'

And so, just like when I went to buy my first house, I decided that I would learn as much as possible about yoga and meditation. To my dismay, I found that, unlike anything else I had ever studied before, the more I studied, the less I knew! Each piece of knowledge I gained merely unearthed an entirely new and hitherto unexplored subject area. Yoga led to Buddhist philosophy, which led to meditation, mindfulness, neuroscience, neuroplasticity and even quantum physics. I could spend the rest of my life studying this and still not know anything. The idea thrilled me.

I turned my newfound interest into a job (as usual), teaching mindfulness and yoga classes, and even getting booked to teach at a few different retreat centers overseas. I was trying to scrape together some semblance of a life, something that I 'did'. It was actually a relief, being able to say 'yoga teacher' rather than 'pole dancer or 'stripper' when asked what it was I 'did'. I realise that, even though my new profession comes with its own expectations and assumptions attached to it, at least there were no more raised eyebrows, derogatory comments or unexpected feminist debates over my choice of career. I had started stripping when I was seventeen – just over seventeen years ago. I had now been stripping and swinging around poles for long as I had not. However much I might now try to 'step out empty' into each moment, my tolerance for negative comments about either the pole or stripping industries was zero.

Eager to delve further into who I was, who I had been seventeen years ago before Suzie was 'born', I began to look back through old diaries and journals. I wanted to find out where Suzie had come from and where Emma had gone. I started by reconnecting with the different circles of friends and activities I had let go of during my time with Toby – we had been so caught up doing duo things, I had lost touch with many of the things that I enjoyed doing solo.

I took myself off to a 'Stitch and Hitch' session at Studio Kink. You can either do handy crafts or a form of rope bondage, known as 'Shibari'. I sat down with my cross-stitch beside a girl in a wheelchair. We chatted, compared stitching techniques, ate scones and sipped tea, while a skinny Asian man in suspenders and high heels was tied up beside us in intricate rope bondage. The contrast was beautiful. The girl in the wheelchair told me she went to BDSM nightclubs because she can't go to 'normal' nightclubs.

'Yeah, I love dancing, but people deliberately bump into me or ask me, 'What's the point?''

'What's the point?'

'Of me, in my chair, going to a place where people dance.'

I looked over at the cross-stitch she was working on.

It said: 'Because that's how I roll.'

I was filled with a mix of anger at the morons who insulted her and a growing sense of admiration. This girl was awesome.

From my time with the 'geeks'n'freaks' at school to the BDSM community and the alternative stripping scene, I've always gravitated towards the fringe because, like the girl in the wheelchair, that was where I found a complete lack of judgement and unconditional acceptance. I realised how much I missed the open-mindedness of this community. There were no derogatory comments about my job; I was just accepted for who I was.

I booked myself a solo show spot back at the BDSM club, Hellfire. It had been almost ten years since I had last graced that stage. I finally had the open and honest relationship with my family that I had longed for. I told my Dad about the upcoming show.

'Be careful Em, they're all sexual deviants there.'

I paused and took a breath before responding. Mindfulness in action.

'Actually Dad, they're not. Around that scene, I have never once been disrespected, objectified or felt unsafe. Whereas I have very much felt those things in normal pubs and clubs.'

'Really? I had no idea.'

Tempted to tell him 'Don't knock it 'til you've tried it,' instead I added, 'Besides, where else would let me to do a strip show as Elsa from *Frozen*?'

I took my clothes off on a Friday night, as a Disney princess in a blonde wig, silver cape and shiny blue dress to the strains of 'Let it Go'.

I walked in to teach my mindfulness class the following Monday. Two of my students came up to me and said, 'We loved your show at Hellfire on Friday.'

My blood ran cold and I stared at them, wide-eyed. That which I had most feared most, and had tried to avoid for so long, had finally happened. The worlds of Emma and Suzie had just collided spectacularly and it was … okay. No thunderbolts, no lightning. Just an group of expectant faces, waiting for me to lead them in a guided meditation.

…

Life went on and I kept uncovering Emma. I booked in with a photographer to do a nude shoot, not as Suzie, but as Emma. No make-up artist. No fake tan. Not pretending to be a glamour model. Not arching my back and pulling orgasm faces. It was just me, naked, in the bushland out the back of my parents' house. I climbed trees and sat in muddy puddles and threw sticks to distract my dog (who had decided to join us) so the photographer could snap the shot. It was wonderful. I felt alive. I felt natural and beautiful. I felt like … me.

The Suzie Switch was off. It was a blessed relief.

It had become really tiring pretending to be someone else for so long. Now it was time to …

Oh God, I realised, *I'm trying to 'find myself.'*

Oh well, if I couldn't buy a sports car and date a stripper, I would do the next most obvious thing …

I booked myself a flight to India, the spiritual capital of the world. The country that would let my spirit breathe and would, apparently, give me what I needed (which may or may not be what I wanted). I booked myself to stay at an ashram, a place dedicated to spiritual study and humanitarian efforts, and got in trouble almost immediately because my ankles were showing. It was like being back at private school. I wasn't prancing through the meditation hall in a bikini. I was wearing a sleeved tunic that fell below my knees and baggy pants (that also fell just below my knees).

'You should see what I used to wear!' I muttered under my breath. I was a little surprised at how grumpy the woman was. The purpose of all this spiritual stuff was simply to 'be happy now', wasn't it? Quite a few of the people there seemed a little ... stressed.

A few years ago, my mom had said to me that stress was a choice. It absolutely infuriated me at the time. Did she seriously think I would choose to be so anxious and stressed out? Would anyone choose to be this way? She didn't understand my schedule, the pressure I was under, how busy I was. At that time, I'd fantasise about quitting everything and going to live in an ashram, away from normal society and the pressures of everyday life. Meals provided to me three time each day and nothing to do, except sit and meditate, maybe having the odd philosophical discussion with the other people. It would be so easy to be stress-free when you didn't have anything to stress about.

Except, I noticed something interesting about some (not all) of the long-term ashram dwellers. It was as if their ability to handle stress had actually decreased. They were all peace and bliss when meditating, but if you cut the potatoes the wrong way, or changed the kitchen roster last minute – look out. The people living in the ashram had dedicated their lives to their spiritual practice. Removing themselves from the 'matrix' of the real world, only to be in another kind of matrix. They woke at 5 a.m. each day in order to practice meditation and chanting but wouldn't return my smiles as I passed them, or were distracted when I engaged them in conversation, swapping one lot of perceived stressors for another. Despite my earlier desires to run away from it all, after seeing what life there was really like, I didn't feel like it was my path to withdraw completely from society (okay, maybe just for a little while). Ultimately, I hoped my meditation and mindfulness practice would prepare me for re-entry into normal society. I now agreed with my mom; stress is a choice – but only if you have access to the personal resources to be able to recognise it as such.

Spiritual practices can be one such resource. They can be beautiful, magical experiences that leave you feeling connected to your higher self, nature and the whole Universe. They can also become like a checklist, where if something disturbs your ticking, you're thrown off-center. Some of the *kriyas* (cleansing practices) at the ashram were not for me – neti pots were okay (pouring salt water into one nostril so it flowed out the other) but I drew the line at *kunjal*, which involved drinking two litres of salt water then sticking your fingers down your throat until you cleared the contents of your stomach by vomiting.

Almost anything in life can become a spiritual practice if you do it with full awareness, but if you find you're still getting thrown out of your center easily – if other people's words or actions are causing you distress – then perhaps you need to reconsider. When my boss criticised me for eating before teaching yoga, I hung onto his words. I took them with me into my class and probably clung to them for the remainder of the day (or even longer), sharing with anyone who'd listen how much I thought I was 'right' and he was 'wrong'. Passing judgement on him for passing judgement on me. Rather than simply Ganeshing that shit and either talking to him about it, or letting go of the issue altogether. Maybe a weekly *kunjal* would have helped me Ganesh shit more easily? I don't know.

Perhaps the people I met in the ashram were just having an off day; maybe they really were happy inside and maybe they weren't even that grumpy, it was just my perception of them. But I couldn't help but compare them to other people in my life, who weren't necessarily 'spiritual' but who consistently greeted each day with joy and happiness. Like Toby. I missed Toby. We had been apart for more than twelve months now.

I pulled myself out of my Toby daydreams, which were frequent and persistent, especially when I was supposed to be meditating, and back into the present. Climbing aboard a twenty-hour lumbering overnight train, I huddled among the luggage on the top rack of a sleeper carriage, while the Indian men underneath me passed up pieces of sugary bread and cups of hot chai. I arrived at 5 a.m. in a beachside village. I snuck into the yoga studio I was going to be training at, and fell asleep on some dirty yoga mats on the roof. At 9 a.m., the teacher woke me.

'You're up late,' I murmured sleepily, I was used to the 5 a.m. wake-up call in the ashram.

'I am vampire,' he grinned, with his crooked smile and signature Indian head-wobble.

There was a cigarette hanging from one corner of his mouth and a piece of fabric wrapped around his wiry mid-section, just covering his privates (although not so much when he was in certain yoga poses) and tucking into his butt crack like a G-string. No problems having my ankles out here. I could have rocked up in a pole training outfit (hot pants and crop top) and he'd have thought it was great. He had holes in the soles of his feet because he'd never worn shoes, he had lived in a cave in the Himalayas for several years and he had studied under Pattabhi Jois (the creator of Vinyasa/Ashtanga yoga) for almost twenty years. He guzzled red wine every other evening, while telling me that smoking weed and drinking were important parts of a 'yogic lifestyle'. I liked him. He seemed to be having much more fun than the people in the Ashram.

I spent two weeks training with him on his rooftop. We practiced Ashtanga yoga and he taught me sacred mantras and played singing bowls while I lay down to meditate on dirty mattresses in his dingy house, staring up at the greying and cracked ceiling. It was wonderful. Although I didn't mind the dirty yoga mats and mattresses, I told him I really didn't like squatting to poo over the keyhole toilet, using a cup of water and my hand to clean up afterwards.

He threw his head back and let out a wild laugh. 'Touching your shit transcends your ego! You meant to be yoga teacher! How are you going to teach other people to transcend their ego if you won't touch your shit?'

I went and bought some toilet paper.

On my way back to the yoga center, an overweight Indian man in flowing white robes beckoned me over. He was a swami (Hindu religious teacher). I knew this because it was written in bold lettering on a sign with his picture on it, nailed up to the wall behind him.

'Come. Sit with me. One minute.'

I didn't want to be rude, especially not to a swami – after all, I was here to learn about spirituality. Maybe he would teach me something? So I sat down beside him in a plastic chair (setting my precious toilet paper carefully underneath), protected from the hot Indian Sun by the dappled shade of a tree. His eyes were almost black, set like little currants into the doughy folds of his brown face. He smelled pleasant, a mix of sandalwood and soap.

'I show you touching meditation.'

He took hold of my hand with one of his and began to caress my fingers and arm with the other. His skin was rough and calloused. It felt scratchy on my arm.

'This is touching meditation,' he said. 'Just feel

241

sensations and disconnect from thoughts.'

I was mostly thinking, *This is weird, and slightly creepy*, but I did as he said and tried to disconnect. After about ten minutes, he ceased his stroking and, still keeping a firm grip on my hand, he told me he wanted to practice tantric sex with me.

'There can be no boundaries between us.'

I stared at him quizzically and raised one eyebrow.

'If there are boundaries, you are saying there is a distinction between us. You are not acknowledging that we are one. You cannot refuse me anything. Because we are one.'

This sounded an awful lot like non-consensual sex to me.

At least when I was a stripper, I was paid to deal with this kind of rubbish. *Dammit, where was Suzie Q when I needed her?* I extracted my hand, picked up my toilet paper and left. I was pretty sure that this was an offer he made only to western girls travelling alone. I was willing to bet he had some 'boundaries' around practicing with men.

I felt mildly nauseated at the thought of sex with him but, what disturbed me the most, was that his argument was spiritually sound. Almost all spiritual teachings come back to the point that there is no 'me', no 'you', no separation between 'us' and 'that'. But using that concept to try and have sex with people? I felt like The Club was more honest with its transactional approach to sexuality. The interaction with the Swami was the end of India for me. I was tired of curries and cold showers, tired of being offered 'Tantra massages' from 'gurus' and

Chapter 12

I was *really* tired of always having dirty feet.

...

I leave India and make my way back to work at the retreat center in Bali. It's now almost two years since I was here with Toby, but I still feel his presence everywhere. Vivid memories come flooding back when I see places we'd eaten together, laughed together. Tears come into my eyes as we pass the workshop where he'd spent two days carving an Om symbol out of coconut shell for me. I brush thoughts of him aside. I am here to work. I will focus on that.

Whereas during my previous stint at the retreat center I taught as Suzie, this time I ask to be called Emma. This causes considerable confusion among the staff; they eventually settle on 'Squemma'. I like it. It's a nice mix of Emma and Suzie Q. It feels good to be back in Bali. Walking through the verdant rice fields and inhaling the clean air, I can feel the tingling and aliveness in my body. Since my time in Vipassana, I am more aware than ever of even the smallest bodily sensation. I'm not sure if I will ever be able to bend twirl and bend a fork like Richard could, but I can notice the physical sensations that go along with the emotions of anxiety, anger, love and peace. And from the brutal boot camp of Vipassana, I also know that whatever sensations I am experiencing, however intense (even haemorrhoid-intense), they will soon pass.

My first night back, I take part in an *Agnihotra* fire ceremony. Fire is usually seen as destructive, but this ceremony focuses on its transformative qualities. All the retreat guests and staff have gathered around a flaming pyramid of cow dung covered in clarified butter. (Yeah – some of this spiritual stuff still seems a little weird.) We chant mantras and, one by one, we kneel in front of the flames and make an offering to the fire. Your offering is something that you want to transform in your life. *Alright,* I think to myself, perhaps a little smugly. *I'll submit Suzie Q to the fire.*

I sweep my long white skirt dramatically out of the way as I kneel in front of the poo-inferno. I mentally thank Suzie for her strength, her courage, for protecting me and keeping me safe for all these years.

'But,' I whisper, 'It's my turn. I've got this now.'

Although I see Suzie as strong and Emma as weak, the fact is, I am only one person and whatever strength 'Suzie' has, actually comes from me. I smile to myself at this realisation and, after the ceremony finishes, I return to my small room feeling more at peace with the world and with myself.

Then my peaceful feeling starts to feel more like queasiness. Then outright nausea.

I run outside and fall onto my hands and knees in the grass.

I vomit.

And vomit.

And vomit.

I stop for about half an hour, then vomit again.

I'm worried. The last time this happened, I ended up in hospital, and right now I'm a long, long way from any kind of western medicine.

At 3 a.m. my boss summons the local healer. My eyes flutter open as I see the dark shape of the small Balinese man moving around the base of my bed.

'What's he going to do? Make a dance for me?' I croak. I feel sick, weak and sarcastic.

The healer places his hands on my feet.

'You just eniji,' he said, 'I just eniji.'

'Energy?' I asked.

'Now I give you eniji.'

It sounds weird, but I feel a sense of calm spread upwards from my feet through my entire body. It feels like I'm being poured full of warm honey.

I don't vomit again.

I don't know if it was a well-timed stomach bug or a spectacular farewell to Suzie Q. Burnt in a fire then thrown up into the garden.

And the toilet.

And a bucket.

A dramatic end for a dramatic showgirl. She had come from inside me, she had come out from inside of me, literally. And now she is gone.

I wake up the next day, feeling fine. The 'sit-and-keep-quiet' meditation teacher asks how I'm feeling.

'Good,' I reply, 'sort of ... peaceful.'

'You are peaceful.'

My eyes widen. What? No one has ever used that word to describe me, ever. Maybe he can see something in me that I can't?

'You teach yoga, don't you? Meditation?'

'Yes.'

'Then you lead people to their peaceful center. You can't give people something you don't have yourself.'

'But I'm having serious trouble reconciling this "Om Shanti Shanti lifestyle" with my need to achieve all the things. Do all the things.'

'The difficulty is, you are in fact two people.'

No kidding. 'But which one is real?'

'Which one do you want to be?'

'Both.' And it's true. I want both. I miss performing. At night I put on music and dance around the empty shala, doing shows for no one, for myself.

'It's hard, but it's possible to have both. You just can't be too attached to either identity.'

'But what do I do?'

'Do nothing. Just sit and keep quiet. Your true value lies in being, not in doing. In fact, by not doing you create space for things to arise on their own. Without any effort from you.'

During our next meditation session together, I try it. I sit quietly.

Who am I? I ask silently.

The answer comes slowly. In the same way the Sun was breaking over the horizon, it dawned on me that I am, in fact, both Emma and Suzie.

And the same time, I'm actually neither; they are both just created identities.

'I' exist in the space in between.

I can feel the physical softening in my body when I surrender to that space of nothingness. I can physically feel how much less resistance there is when I stop pushing.

I have a week off at the end of my contract with the retreat center so I send Toby a text:

What would you say if I asked you to fly over to Bali?

I close my eyes, cross my fingers and hit send. I don't even wait for a response. I added:

Am I 'Universing' or just pushing like usual?

I watch the little bouncing dots in eager anticipation of his reply:

Maybe somewhere in the middle?

The middle way, it's always the middle way.

He adds:

Was that a hypothetical question?

No, it was not hypothetical.

My phone dings as another message comes through. *Penthouse* magazine is interested in publishing my 'naked in the bush' shoot. My Emma shoot. The one where I was not trying to be sexy; the one where I was not really trying at all. They have stopped referring to their models as 'Pets'. No longer do they want shots of 'fake girls in bubble-gum bikinis batting false lashes with manufactured personalities' (their words). They now want models who are real. Who are naturally beautiful, healthy and confident. Who are comfortable in their own skin.

How perfect.

Everything that is happening is perfect. You are perfect. The only thing that is ever not perfect is your thinking about yourself.

Things really do arise out of nothingness when I stop

trying so hard. It's like we are riding this golden flow of energy that's twisting and turning through invisible corridors and rooms, as it carries us through our lives. Sometimes it will pass an open doorway that we really, really want to enter and we'll reach out with both arms and cling on by our fingernails. It will be hard and it won't feel good, because the energy is trying to guide us forward to something else. And, eventually, we will be forced to let go of things that were not meant for us. Sometimes it will feel like we are stopped, stuck in a dead-end passageway, but we are never truly stopped – the energy will eventually find a small crack in a low corner that it can squeeze through. We just need to trust enough to be able to let go and do nothing.

I'm not quite Suzie anymore, but I'm not quite Emma either. The pendulum swung all the way over to Suzie, then all the way over to Emma. Now it needs to stop somewhere in the middle. The middle way.

Toby will be here soon. Before he gets here, I might see about changing my voicemail message.

I'm thinking 'Hi, you've reached Squemma.'

Thank you to ...

'You're only as good as the people around you.' Thankfully, I had a lot of amazing people around me as I wrote this book. A huge thanks to all of them. Starting with my parents, especially Mum, who has had to deal with so many 'evolutions' of Emma. From dating girls, to being a stripper, to wandering around the world as a barefoot hippie, she has always loved me just as I am. Thank you to my dad for continuously reminding me to prioritise my 'physical and mental health' over all else and reminding me, repeatedly, that I am, in fact, the one in control of my destiny. Also, to my step parents Dave and Karen for their support and love. To my little sister Catherine – you are more of an inspiration than you will ever know. Amber, Zahra and Missy – for the 'Recovering Strippers Support Group' #startwithcoffee. And Toby J, Mr MacGyver, you really are capable of anything. To Charlee for helping me turn Suzie Q Pole Studio from an idea on a pool table at a swingers club into the empire it became. Mr Buddhism for introducing me to Mindfulness in the first place and to Veronica for telling me to stop listening to him and 'just write'. To Jannine – for endless cups of tea, honest chats and unwavering support. To Logan and Beth, the sunshine and peace to my fire. To my amazing initial editor Sharon and also to Pol Marias for showing me the value of an editor in the first place. Lars, if it weren't for you, the elephant would still be trapped in the clay. Thank you for believing in me. Finally, to my teacher Panda Chi, you taught me 'nothing' and for that I am extremely grateful.

Although the events described are real some chronology has also been changed for the sake of the narrative. In this book the names of some of the people and businesses referenced have been altered to protect their privacy.

www.suzieq.com.au

First published in 2018 by New Holland Publishers
London • Sydney • Auckland

131-151 Great Titchfield Street, London WIW 5BB, United Kingdom
1/66 Gibbes Street, Chatswood, NSW 2067, Australia
5/39 Woodside Ave, Northcote, Auckland 0627, New Zealand

newhollandpublishers.com

A record of this book is held at the British Library and the National Library
of Australia.

ISBN 9781742579986

Group Managing Director: Fiona Schultz
Publisher: Alan Whiticker
Project Editor: Jess Cox
Proofreader: Kaitlyn Smith
Designer: Catherine Meachen
Production Director: James Mills-Hicks
Printer: Hang Tai Printing Company Limited

10 9 8 7 6 5 4 3 2 1

Keep up with New Holland Publishers on Facebook
facebook.com/NewHollandPublishers

UK £12.99
US $24.99